FLORIDA BUCKET LIST

Explore Hidden Gems and Iconic Destinations. Turn Your Dreams into Reality While Creating Lifelong Memories (Includes Interactive Map)

Dylan and Rachel Marston

© Copyright 2024 Dylan and Rachel Marston All rights reserved

© Copyright 2024 Dylan and Rachel Marston All rights reserved

Copyrights Notice

No part of this book may be reproduced in any form or by any electronic or mechanical means, including information storage and retrieval systems, without written permission from the author.

Recording of this publication is strictly prohibited and any storage of this document is not allowed unless with written permission from the publisher.

All rights reserved. Respective authors own all copyrights not held by the publisher.

Pictures inside this book are of the respective owners, granted to the Author in a Royalty-Free license.

All trademarks, service marks, product names, and the characteristics of any names mentioned in this book are considered the property of their respective owners and are used only for reference. No endorsement is implied when we use one of these terms.

Limited Liability

Please note that the content of this book is based on personal experience and various information sources, and it is only for personal use.

Please note the information contained within this document is for educational and entertainment purposes only and no warranties of any kind are declared or implied.

Readers acknowledge that the author is not engaging in the rendering of legal, financial or professional advice. Please consult a licensed professional before attempting any techniques outlined in this book.

Nothing in this book is intended to replace common sense or legal accounting, or professional advice and is meant only to inform.

Your particular circumstances may not be suited to the example illustrated in this book; in fact, they likely will not be.

You should use the information in this book at your own risk. The reader is responsible for his or her actions.

The information provided herein is stated to be truthful and consistent, in that any liability, in terms of inattention or otherwise, by any usage or abuse of any policies, processes, or directions contained within is the solitary and utter responsibility of the recipient reader.

By reading this book, the reader agrees that under no circumstances is the author responsible for any losses, direct or indirect, which are incurred as a result of the use of the information contained within this document, including, but not limited to, errors, omissions, or inaccuracies.

Table of Contents

INTRODUCTION 7
ABOUT FLORIDA 9
Landscape 9
Climate 12
Flora and Fauna 15
Florida History 19
NORTHWEST FLORIDA 31
Beaches 31
A Journey Through Time and Culture 38
Three-Day Itinerary for Northwest Florida: The Panhandle 44
NORTHEAST FLORIDA 49
Must-see tourist attractions 51
A Perfect Day in St. Augustine 54
A Day Immersed in Jacksonville's Vibrant Arts Scene 56
A Day Exploring Amelia Island's Charming Coastal Retreats ... 59
Hidden Gem Itinerary for Northeast Florida 62
CENTRAL FLORIDA 67
Interesting Places to Visit 69
Orlando: Best Theme Park Experience 71
Orlando's best authentic experiences 74
Orlando's Best Restaurants 78
Orlando's Best Hotels 83
Lesser-known Gems in Central Florida 88
Orlando in Three Days 91

THE SPACE COAST 97
One-Day Itinerary in Cape Canaveral.................................... 100
Three-Day Itinerary: Hidden Gems of The Space Coast 104
SOUTH FLORIDA 109
Exploring Miami... 111
Must-Visit Cities in South Florida 115
FINAL THOUGHTS 129

INTRODUCTION

Welcome to the Florida Bucket List, your ultimate guide to 120 extraordinary adventures across the Sunshine State. Whether you're a local rediscovering your home or a first-time visitor, this book leads you to Florida's best blend of nature, culture, and excitement, showcasing the most stunning and memorable spots.

Imagine enjoying a Gulf Coast sunset, snorkeling through coral reefs, or exploring historic forts where Florida's rich past comes to life. From pristine beaches and lush parks to thrilling attractions, Florida offers something for everyone—beach lovers, history enthusiasts, nature admirers, and adventure seekers.

This guide goes beyond popular attractions, offering vivid descriptions, precise addresses, and all the essential details to ensure your seamless trip. Whether it's peaceful beaches, lively boardwalks, or cultural landmarks, this book helps you create unforgettable memories.

Each destination in this book has been carefully curated to include all the necessary details, ensuring you can plan your adventure effortlessly and make the most of your trip. Whether you're a first-time visitor or a seasoned Floridian, this guide provides you with everything you need to explore Florida's wonders with ease.

In summary in this guide you will find:

Accurate Description of Each Destination: Each location is paired with an engaging, detailed description to paint a vivid picture of what you can expect. These descriptions help you understand the unique appeal of each spot—whether it's the tranquil ambiance of a secluded beach, the thrilling excitement of a theme park, or the historical richness of a cultural landmark.

Nearest City: For clarity, each destination includes the closest major city, giving you a clear reference point and helping you understand its position relative to Florida's key urban centers.

GPS Coordinates: To ensure a smooth journey, we provide precise GPS coordinates for each destination, allowing you to input them directly into your device for quick and easy navigation.

Best Time to Visit: Each destination also includes recommendations for the ideal times to visit—whether it's to avoid peak crowds, experience perfect weather, or witness a location at its most captivating.

Tolls and Access Fees: All relevant information on tolls, parking fees, and entry charges are included, so you'll be fully prepared for any costs and avoid surprises along the way.

Did You Know? Every destination features fascinating facts or historical tidbits, offering you additional insights to enrich your visit. These fun details bring each place to life and provide a deeper connection to your adventure.

Website: We've included links to the official websites of each destination, so you can stay up-to-date with the latest information or check for last-minute changes to your plans.

Interactive state map: This digital tool allows you to visualize your route, plan your journey, and explore specific regions with ease. Whether you're planning a structured road trip or diving deeper into a particular area, the map will keep you organized and help you get the most out of your trip.

With everything you need to explore Florida's most exciting and memorable destinations at your fingertips, you're ready to set off on an unforgettable adventure.

ABOUT FLORIDA

Landscape

Florida is a state of incredible diversity when it comes to its landscapes. Whether you're hiking through tropical rainforests, relaxing on sugar-sand beaches, or exploring expansive wetlands, Florida offers a breathtaking array of natural environments that will captivate any traveler. The Sunshine State's landscapes stretch from the colorful coastlines of the Atlantic and Gulf of Mexico to the untouched beauty of Everglades National Park. It is a place where every region has its unique charm, making Florida a must-see destination for anyone interested in the wonders of nature.

Coastal Beauty

Florida's coastline is world-renowned, and for good reason. With over 1,300 miles of shoreline, it boasts some of the most beautiful beaches in the world. The pristine white sands of the Gulf Coast stretch from the quiet shores of Sanibel Island to the lively beaches of Destin, while the Atlantic Coast offers vibrant beach towns like Miami Beach, Daytona Beach, and the islands of the Florida Keys. Each coastal area provides its distinct vibe, from the calm, turquoise waters of the Gulf to the crashing waves of the Atlantic, making Florida a paradise for sun-seekers and water sports enthusiasts alike.

Wetlands and Everglades

Moving inland, the Everglades—the largest tropical wilderness in the U.S.—offers an entirely different experience. These wetlands, made up of slow-moving rivers and vast marshes, are home to an astonishing variety of wildlife, including alligators, manatees, and over 350 species of birds. A tour through the Everglades is like stepping into another world, where the landscape shifts dramatically from dense mangroves to sawgrass prairies, and where the serenity of the water is only interrupted by the occasional splash of a jumping fish. Beyond the Everglades, Florida is also home to other unique wetlands, such as the Big Cypress National Preserve, where swampy landscapes meet ancient cypress trees and an array of wildlife.

Florida's Diverse Forests

Florida also boasts an impressive array of forests. The state is home to the longleaf pine forests that once covered much of the southeastern U.S. These forests are a critical habitat for numerous species, such as the red-cockaded woodpecker and the eastern indigo snake. On a visit to places like the Apalachicola National Forest or the Ocala National Forest, travelers can hike through towering pine trees, explore springs that bubble up from deep underground or enjoy the stillness of nature in one of the most biodiverse ecosystems in the U.S.

Inland Lakes and Springs

Florida's inland areas are dotted with sparkling lakes, rivers, and springs that provide tranquil escapes for those looking to paddle, fish, or simply soak in the beauty of the landscape. The freshwater springs of central Florida, such as Wakulla Springs and Silver Springs, are some of the largest and clearest in the world. These crystal-clear waters have been a key attraction for visitors for centuries, offering the chance to see manatees, otters, and even the occasional alligator in their natural habitat.

Florida is also known for its inland lakes, which are particularly abundant in the central and northern parts of the state. Lake Okeechobee, the largest freshwater lake in the state, is a vast and scenic landscape where travelers can enjoy boating, bird watching, and even experience local wildlife like bald eagles and wild hogs. The lake also plays a significant role in Florida's water management system, feeding the Everglades and providing a vital water source to the entire state.

Islands and Keys

The Florida Keys, a chain of islands stretching out into the warm waters of the Gulf of Mexico, is another iconic landscape that draws visitors from around the world. The vibrant coral reefs surrounding the Keys are a haven for snorkelers and divers, while the islands themselves offer lush tropical environments and laid-back, island living. The drive across the Overseas Highway provides some of the most dramatic and scenic coastal views in the U.S., with turquoise waters on both sides and small islands in the distance.

Mountains and High Terrain

Although Florida is known for its flatness, there are small hills and elevated areas that offer a different perspective on the state's landscape. The Lake Wales Ridge is the highest point in peninsular Florida and provides a unique mix of pine forests and scrubby terrain. While it may not have the towering mountain ranges of other states, the ridge offers rolling hills and unique ecosystems that are worth exploring for those interested in the state's topography and biodiversity.

Climate

Florida's climate is one of the most appealing and unique aspects of the state, drawing millions of visitors each year seeking sunshine and warmth. However, the state's weather isn't just about endless summer days; it offers a variety of microclimates and seasonal shifts that make Florida an exciting destination for all types of travelers. Here's a closer look at Florida's climate:

Year-Round Sunshine

Known as the "Sunshine State," Florida lives up to its name with an impressive 230 days of sunshine annually. This abundance of sunny weather makes it a perfect spot for year-round outdoor adventures and activities.

The northern part of the state typically experiences mild winters, while southern Florida enjoys a tropical climate, perfect for those who want to escape colder northern temperatures. Even during the winter months, temperatures rarely drop below 50°F (10°C), making it an attractive getaway for snowbirds.

Tropical Climate in the South

Southern Florida, including the Florida Keys and Miami, has a tropical climate. The area experiences warm temperatures year-round, with average highs ranging from 75°F (24°C) in winter to 90°F (32°C) in summer. Humidity is a constant feature in the south, and while rainfall can occur year-round, the wettest months are from June to September, which coincides with the Atlantic hurricane season. Although this region enjoys balmy weather, occasional summer thunderstorms can bring sudden but brief downpours, followed by clear skies.

Subtropical Climate in the Central Region

In central Florida, cities like Orlando and Tampa experience a subtropical climate. Summers are long, hot, and humid, with afternoon thunderstorms a regular occurrence, while winters are relatively mild. The temperatures in winter tend to stay in the 60s and 70s°F (15-25°C), and summer highs can reach the low 90s°F (32-34°C). This region is particularly well-suited for year-round outdoor activities, from theme parks to water sports, as even the cooler months still offer plenty of sunshine.

Temperate Climate in the North

Northern Florida, including cities like Jacksonville and Tallahassee, has a more temperate climate. Winters can get cooler, with temperatures occasionally dipping below freezing in the northernmost parts. The summer season is characterized by high temperatures, heavy humidity, and frequent afternoon thunderstorms. This area is the perfect destination for those who prefer a more varied climate with distinct seasons, including the occasional chill of winter that adds to the diversity of outdoor experiences.

Hurricane Season

While Florida is blessed with a mostly warm and sunny climate, it also faces the threat of hurricanes and tropical storms, particularly in the summer and fall. The official hurricane season runs from June through November, with the highest frequency of storms occurring from August to October. These storms bring heavy rains, strong winds, and the possibility of coastal flooding, especially in southern and central Florida. However, the state has robust emergency preparedness systems in place, and many travelers consider Florida's storm season as part of the adventure It's always a good idea to stay informed about current weather conditions and plan accordingly to ensure a safe and enjoyable experience.

Rainfall and Humidity

Florida's rainfall is another defining feature of its climate. The state sees an average annual rainfall of about 50 inches (127 cm), with the highest amounts recorded in the summer months due to thunderstorms. The central and southern regions are particularly prone to intense rainfall during the summer afternoon hours, while northern Florida experiences more evenly distributed rainfall throughout the year. Humidity, too, plays a big role, especially in summer. While the heat can be intense, the humidity often makes it feel even warmer, particularly in the southern parts of the state.

Best Times to Visit

The best times to visit Florida depend largely on the kind of experience you're seeking. For ideal weather and fewer crowds, the spring (March to May) and fall (September to November) months are often recommended. During these times, temperatures are pleasant, and there's a lower chance of rain. The summer months (June to August) are typically hot and humid, with higher chances of rain, though the beaches and theme parks are still bustling with tourists.

If you prefer fewer crowds and milder temperatures, plan your trip during the winter months (December to February), especially if you're traveling to the southern regions, where the weather remains warm and pleasant. However, be mindful of the increased number of snowbirds—many visitors from colder northern regions flock to Florida during this time, especially in cities like Miami and Sarasota.

Flora and Fauna

Florida's flora and fauna are among the most diverse and abundant in the United States, thanks to the state's unique mix of tropical and temperate climates. This biodiversity is not only visually stunning but also plays a crucial role in maintaining the ecological balance of the state. From the lush mangrove swamps of the Everglades to the pine forests of the Panhandle, Florida offers a wide range of habitats that are home to an impressive array of plant and animal species.

Flora: A Verdant Tapestry

Florida's plant life is as diverse as its landscapes. The state is home to over 4,000 species of plants, many of which are found nowhere else in the world. Here are some highlights:

Tropical and Subtropical Plants

In the southern parts of Florida, particularly in the Florida Keys and Everglades, you'll find an abundance of tropical plants. These include lush palms like the Cabbage Palm (Florida's state tree) and the Royal Palm, as well as the towering Cypress trees and dense mangrove swamps. Mangroves are vital to Florida's coastal ecosystems, providing shelter for young fish and other marine life.

Bromeliads, vibrant flowering plants that grow in humid environments, are commonly seen, along with hibiscus, bougainvillea, and various species of orchids. These plants, often brightly colored, thrive in Florida's tropical climate.

Coastal and Wetland Flora

Florida's wetlands and coastal areas are home to an array of salt-tolerant plants. Sawgrass, a tall marsh grass, is a defining feature of the Everglades. Other wetland plants like Water Lilies and Pickerelweed provide food and shelter to a variety of wildlife, from insects to larger mammals.

The coastal dunes are home to sea oats, which help stabilize the sand and prevent erosion. The sea grape, a sprawling shrub with large, round leaves, is common along the shorelines of the Gulf Coast and the Atlantic.

Pine Forests and Oak Hammocks

The central and northern parts of Florida are characterized by dense pine forests and oak hammocks. Longleaf Pines are one of the most iconic species in these areas, and the slash pine is another common sight. These forests host a mix of shrubs, including gallberry bushes and wax myrtle.

Fauna: The Wild Side of Florida

Florida is a haven for wildlife, with species adapted to a wide variety of ecosystems, from its tropical swamps to its dry uplands. The state is known for its unique and often rare animal species, and many of these creatures are protected due to their endangered status.

Mammals

Florida is home to a variety of mammals, ranging from the small Eastern Cottontail Rabbit to the larger Florida Panther, an endangered species that resides in the swamps and forests of southern Florida. The Manatee, also known as the sea cow, is another iconic animal of Florida. These gentle giants are often seen grazing in the warm waters of the Gulf Coast, especially in winter when they seek out warmer areas near natural springs.

The White-tailed Deer and Wild Boar are also common in the state, particularly in the more rural regions. Black Bears roam in certain forested parts of Florida, including the Ocala National Forest, one of the largest national forests in the state.

Birds

Florida is a birdwatcher's paradise. Over 500 species of birds either migrate through or call Florida home. Among the most iconic is the

Roseate Spoonbill, with its bright pink feathers, and the Bald Eagle, which nests in Florida's protected areas. The Florida Scrub-Jay, unique to the state and found only in the scrub regions, is another highlight. The state's wetlands, beaches, and forests support many species of waterfowl, shorebirds, and songbirds, making it a key destination for birdwatching.

American Flamingos, although historically rare, are making a comeback in Florida, especially along the southern and eastern coasts. The Great Egret and Wood Stork are also frequently seen in wetlands and estuaries.

Reptiles and Amphibians

Florida is well-known for its reptiles, many of which thrive in its warm, wet environment. The American Alligator is a symbol of the state and can be found in nearly all of Florida's freshwater lakes, rivers, and marshes. The state is also home to the Gopher Tortoise, an important species that digs burrows used by over 350 other species.

Snakes are also common, with the Eastern Diamondback Rattlesnake being one of the most well-known species. The Florida Green Anole, a small lizard that can change color, is often spotted in yards and gardens across the state.

Florida's amphibians, like the Southern Chorus Frog and the Cuban Treefrog, thrive in the state's warm and wet conditions, filling the air with their croaks in the evenings.

Marine Life

Florida's surrounding waters are teeming with marine life, making it a prime destination for divers and ocean enthusiasts. The coral reefs off the coast, particularly in the Florida Keys, support a wealth of species, including the Loggerhead Turtle, Hawksbill Turtle, and Green Sea Turtle. Dolphins, particularly the Bottlenose Dolphin, are commonly seen along the coastline.

Florida's waters are also home to several species of sharks, including the Hammerhead Shark, as well as manatees, stingrays, and various types of sea bass, snapper, and tarpon.

Conservation Efforts

Florida's diverse ecosystems and wildlife face threats from development, climate change, and invasive species Preserving Florida's rich biodiversity is essential, making conservation efforts a vital part of protecting its unique ecosystems and wildlife. Programs to protect endangered species like the Florida Panther and the Manatee, along with efforts to restore habitats such as the Everglades, are essential for preserving Florida's natural beauty.

Efforts to combat invasive species, such as the Burmese Python in the Everglades, are also ongoing, as these non-native animals threaten the delicate balance of Florida's ecosystems.

Florida History

Florida's history is as vibrant and fascinating as its landscapes, full of intriguing events, powerful stories, and cultural influences that have shaped the state we know today. From indigenous settlements to European exploration, from colonial power struggles to the birth of tourism, Florida's past is a treasure trove of adventure and discovery. Whether you're drawn to the state's colorful native cultures, its pivotal role in American history, or its unexpected twists and turns, Florida's history offers something for everyone.

The First Floridians: Indigenous Peoples

Long before European explorers set foot on Florida's shores, the land was home to a variety of Native American tribes, each with its unique culture. The Tequesta people lived along the southeastern coast, while the Calusa, who are perhaps the most well-known of Florida's native groups, ruled the southwestern peninsula. These groups were skilled fishermen and developed advanced methods of boatbuilding and tools, leaving behind fascinating archaeological sites, including shell mounds and burial grounds.

Florida's history is also defined by its Seminole people, who resisted European colonization and fought several wars to retain their territory. The Second Seminole War (1835–1842) is particularly notable, as it became one of the longest and costliest Indian conflicts in American history, marking a key moment in Florida's resistance to outside control.

The Spanish Discovery: The Fountain of Youth and St. Augustine

In 1513, Juan Ponce de León arrived on Florida's shores, famously searching for the Fountain of Youth, though it's uncertain if he ever actually believed it existed. His expedition marked the onset of a significant Spanish influence in Florida. In 1565, the Spanish established the first enduring European settlement in the United States at St. Augustine. It remains the oldest continuously inhabited

European-founded settlement in the nation. The city is home to numerous historic landmarks, including the Castillo de San Marcos, a 17th-century fort that survived several sieges and became a powerful symbol of Spanish fortitude.

During the 17th century, Florida was caught in the crossfire of European colonial rivalries, with Spain and France vying for control. Fort Caroline, founded by the French in 1564 near present-day Jacksonville, was one such outpost, but it was destroyed by the Spanish just two years later. This struggle for dominance set the stage for centuries of conflict over Florida's land.

The British Era: A Short but Impactful Chapter

In the 18th century, Spain ceded Florida to Britain under the Treaty of Paris (1763) after the French and Indian War. The British took control, dividing the territory into East and West Florida. During this time, Florida saw a significant influx of settlers from the British colonies, especially from the Carolinas. However, British control was short-lived. In 1783, as part of the Treaty of Paris following the American Revolution, Britain returned Florida to Spain.

While under British rule, Florida witnessed the rise of plantation agriculture, including the cultivation of indigo, which became a major export. The British also began building more fortified towns and expanded settlements along the coast.

Florida as a U.S. Territory and Statehood

In the early 19th century, tensions in Florida escalated. Spain could no longer maintain control over the territory, which was being used as a haven for pirates, runaway slaves, and hostile Native American tribes. The First Seminole War (1817–1818) saw Andrew Jackson, the future president, invade Florida in pursuit of the Seminole, marking the beginning of a period of American involvement in the state. In 1821, Spain officially transferred control of Florida to the United States, designating it as a U.S. territory.

By 1845, Florida was admitted into the Union as the 27th state, marking its formal inclusion in the United States. The state's economy began to flourish, especially in the production of citrus fruits, sugar, and cotton. The discovery of phosphate in the late 19th century also added to Florida's economic growth, though tensions between the North and South were rising, leading to Florida's secession from the Union in 1861 during the Civil War.

The Post-Civil War Era: Reconstruction and Development

After the Civil War, Florida, like many Southern states, went through a difficult period of Reconstruction. However, the state began to recover in the late 19th century, as new transportation infrastructure such as railroads made it easier to travel to and from the state. The construction of Henry Flagler's East Coast Railway in the 1890s was particularly transformative, opening up the state's beautiful coastline to tourists.

By the early 20th century, Florida began to attract visitors from all over the United States. Flagler also played a major role in the development of Palm Beach and Miami, with the creation of luxurious resorts that drew wealthy visitors.

The Florida Boom and the Birth of Tourism

The early 20th century was a time of incredible transformation. Florida's population exploded during the Florida Land Boom of the 1920s, with developers luring new residents and investors from all over the country. Cities like Miami and Tampa expanded rapidly, though the boom was followed by a sharp bust in 1926, when the stock market crashed, and the real estate market collapsed.

However, the Great Depression did not halt Florida's ascent as a tourist destination. With the opening of iconic resorts, like Walt Disney World in 1971, and the creation of other theme parks, Florida solidified its reputation as the ultimate vacation spot. Disney World in particular became the heart of the state's tourism industry, drawing millions of visitors annually.

Notable Historical Events and Figures

The Cuban Missile Crisis (1962): A tense 13-day confrontation between the United States and the Soviet Union occurred just off the coast of Florida. The event brought the world to the brink of nuclear war and marked a turning point in Cold War politics.

Florida's Space Race: The state's space exploration history is legendary, with Kennedy Space Center serving as the launch site for numerous space missions, including the Apollo moon landings. Florida played a key role in the Cold War-era space race, with its Cape Canaveral launching site being used for historic missions.

Florida Today: A Cultural Melting Pot

Today, Florida's history continues to be defined by its cultural diversity. It is home to a large Hispanic population, particularly in Miami, where Cuban culture has had a profound influence. The state's mix of Latin, African American, and Native American cultures has given rise to a dynamic, diverse population that celebrates everything from festivals to music, art, and food.

Florida's history is more than just a timeline of dates—it's an evolving story that continues to shape the state's identity. From indigenous peoples and European settlers to the booming tourism industry and cultural vibrancy, Florida's history is rich with moments that have left their mark on both the state and the world.

Whether you're wandering through historic districts, visiting battlefields, or exploring cultural landmarks, Florida's past is always just beneath the surface, ready to be discovered and appreciated in new ways.

PLANNING YOUR TRIP TO FLORIDA

Whether you're planning a short getaway or a longer stay, here are some expert tips on how to navigate Florida efficiently, book accommodations, and make the most of your time in the Sunshine State.

1. Navigating Florida's Cities and Highways

Florida's road system is extensive, and it's important to understand the most efficient routes to get around, especially if you're planning to visit multiple cities. Here are some essential points to keep in mind:

Interstate System: The backbone of Florida's highway network is its interstate system. Interstate 95 (I-95) runs along the East Coast, connecting cities like Miami, Fort Lauderdale, and Jacksonville. Interstate 75 (I-75) runs north-south, linking cities such as Naples, Tampa, and Gainesville. These highways are your best bet for quick travel between cities.

Traffic: While Florida's highways are generally well-maintained, traffic congestion can be a challenge, especially in urban areas or during peak tourist seasons (winter and spring). For example, I-4 is notorious for heavy traffic around Orlando, particularly near Walt Disney World and Universal Studios. It's wise to avoid traveling during rush hours (7–9 AM and 4–6 PM) in major cities.

SunPass: To avoid the hassle of stopping to pay tolls, purchase a SunPass. This electronic tolling system works across most of Florida's highways and toll roads, saving you time and hassle. You can buy one at convenience stores, toll plazas, or online.

Public Transportation: While Florida's cities like Miami, Orlando, and Tampa have public transportation options (buses, light rail), many travelers prefer renting a car for the convenience and flexibility to explore off-the-beaten-path destinations. However, do check the availability of rideshare services like Uber or Lyft, which are common in tourist-heavy areas.

2. Booking Accommodations: Where to Stay

Florida is home to a vast range of accommodations, from luxurious resorts to budget-friendly hotels, charming bed and breakfasts, and cozy vacation rentals. Here's how to ensure you make the right choice:

Location is Key: Depending on your itinerary, choosing where to stay can greatly impact your experience. If you're visiting popular cities like Orlando or Miami, staying near major attractions is convenient but often pricey. Opting for accommodations a bit further away from the hotspots (but still within reasonable distance) can save you money and offer a more relaxed atmosphere.

For example, if you're heading to the Everglades, consider staying in **Everglades City** instead of Miami. It's quieter, more affordable, and gives you direct access to nature without the crowds.

Vacation Rentals: Florida is a top destination for vacation rentals, particularly near the coast. Platforms like **Airbnb** and **Vrbo** offer a range of properties—think beach houses, cozy cottages, or even treehouses—that give you a home-like experience. This option is especially attractive for families or groups traveling together, as it provides more space and amenities like kitchens for cooking your meals.

Florida is renowned for its high-end accommodations, featuring world-class resorts like **The Breakers in Palm Beach** and **The Ritz-Carlton in Naples**. These exceptional properties set the standard for luxury, combining elegant surroundings with premier amenities and outstanding service. However, these tend to be expensive, especially during peak season. If you're looking for a more affordable option, there are still many great mid-range hotels that offer excellent amenities at a fraction of the cost.

24

Examples:

Hampton Inn & Suites Orlando-South Lake Buena Vista (near Disney parks) offers convenient access to the parks while providing comfortable accommodations at a moderate price.

For a beach getaway, the **Beachside Hotel and Suites** in Cocoa Beach offers a relaxed, budget-friendly experience without sacrificing quality.

3. Dining: Savoring Florida's Culinary Delights

Florida's dining landscape reflects its rich cultural diversity, with a fusion of Caribbean, Latin American, and Southern influences creating a distinctive culinary experience. From fresh seafood to iconic Cuban cuisine, the state is brimming with unforgettable flavors. Here are some highlights and tips:

Seafood Sensations Florida's reputation as a seafood paradise is well-earned. Signature dishes such as stone crabs, grouper, and Mahi Mahi are beloved by locals and visitors alike. To experience the history and flavor of these dishes, visit renowned spots like **Joe's Stone Crab** in Miami Beach or **The Columbia** in Tampa, the latter known for its Spanish-Cuban heritage and long-standing culinary traditions.

Cuban Cuisine Highlights Miami, particularly the Little Havana neighborhood, boasts some of the best Cuban fare in the U.S. **Versailles Restaurant**, a local institution, serves authentic dishes such as Cuban sandwiches and ropa vieja. A visit here offers not just amazing food but also a glimpse into the cultural heart of the Cuban-American community.

Authentic Local Experiences For a more casual and quintessentially Florida vibe, head to **The Green Parrot Bar** in Key West. Known for its laid-back atmosphere, this iconic spot combines local culture with a menu featuring fresh seafood, Cuban-inspired dishes, and expertly crafted cocktails. Key West's dining scene is a blend of freshness and creativity, making it a must-visit destination for food lovers.

Tips for Enjoying Florida's Cuisine

Eat Local: Seek out small, family-owned eateries and coastal seafood shacks for the freshest flavors.

Time It Right: Plan your visit during stone crab season (October to May) to savor this delicacy at its peak.

Pair Your Meal: Complement Florida's tropical dishes with refreshing cocktails like mojitos, or sample craft beers from one of the state's many breweries.

4. Stress-Free Vacation Tips: Making the Most of Your Time

Plan Ahead: Florida offers so much to see that it can be overwhelming. Consider mapping out your must-see attractions ahead of time. Use a tool like **Google My Maps** or **Roadtrippers** to plan your route and ensure you're not wasting time backtracking.

Pack Smart: Florida's weather is typically warm, but the subtropical climate means you'll want to pack light, breathable clothing. Don't forget sunscreen, a hat, and sunglasses. If you plan on hiking or visiting natural reserves, bring comfortable shoes and bug spray—especially if you're heading to swampy areas like the Everglades.

Hydrate: Florida's humid heat can be draining, so always carry water with you, particularly if you're spending the day outdoors. Many theme parks and nature reserves offer free water refill stations, so keep an eye out.

Time Your Visit: Florida's peak tourist season is from **December to April**, with spring break being particularly busy. If you want to avoid the crowds, visit in the off-season, from **May to November**. While the weather can be hotter, you'll find less congestion and better deals on hotels and attractions.

INTERACTIVE MAPPING PLATFORM

Before you start your journey, we highly recommend accessing the Interactive Mapping Platform by scanning the QR code below. This powerful digital tool is specifically designed to simplify travel planning, helping you navigate your route, explore specific areas, and customize your journey with ease.

This Map provides a user-friendly experience, combining advanced mapping tools with practical travel features. Here's how you can use it effectively to plan and optimize your visit to Florida:

1. Visualize Your Route and Plan Stops

The Map allows you to plot your travel route, identify key attractions, and pinpoint rest stops, restaurants, and landmarks along the way. For example, if you're driving from **Miami to Key West**, you can use the Map to chart a scenic route along the Overseas Highway, highlighting must-see spots like **Islamorada**, the **Seven Mile Bridge**, and local seafood restaurants.

- **Practical Tip**: Use Map's filtering tools to identify gas stations and parking spots for smoother navigation during long drives.

2. Discover Hidden Gems in Specific Regions

The Map goes beyond basic mapping by offering insights into local attractions and hidden treasures. Let's say you're exploring **Naples, Florida**:

- With the Map, you can find recommendations for places like the **Corkscrew Swamp Sanctuary** or the **Naples Pier** and explore less touristy beaches nearby.
- Use the map to locate charming local eateries, such as **The Dock at Crayton Cove** for waterfront dining or a nearby family-owned café for a quick bite.
- **Example**: Type "family-friendly activities near Naples" into Map's search bar to reveal nearby playgrounds, boardwalks, or nature trails.

3. Customize Your Itinerary with Points of Interest

Planning a one-day itinerary in **Orlando**? The Map helps you cluster attractions that are close together, saving time and travel distance. Here's a sample itinerary you can create:

- **Morning**: Start with a visit to **Lake Eola Park** (512 E Washington St, Orlando) for a relaxing stroll and swan boat rides.
- **Lunch**: Find a nearby affordable restaurant using the Map like **Se7en Bites** (617 N Primrose Dr, Orlando) for Southern-style comfort food.
- **Afternoon**: Visit cultural hotspots such as the **Orlando Science Center** or **Harry P. Leu Gardens**.
- **Evening**: Use the Map to locate parking and find dining spots around **International Drive** for dinner with entertainment options like live music.

4. Save Your Favorite Spots

The Map lets you save key locations and build a personalized travel map. For example:

- If you're planning to explore **Fort Lauderdale**, you can save places like **Las Olas Boulevard** for shopping, **Fort Lauderdale Beach** for relaxation, and the **Bonnet House Museum** for history and art.
- **Practical Tip**: Create different categories on you're the Map account, such as "Restaurants," "Activities," and "Hotels," so you can organize your itinerary at a glance.

5. Stay Updated on Real-Time Navigation

The Map also integrates real-time navigation, helping you stay on track during your trip. Whether you're heading to **Everglades National Park** for an airboat tour or driving through the bustling streets of **West Palm Beach**, you'll receive up-to-date directions and traffic alerts.

- **Example**: If there's a delay en route to your sunset celebration in **Key West's Mallory Square**, The Map will suggest alternative routes to ensure you arrive on time.

NORTHWEST FLORIDA

Beaches

Northwest Florida's Panhandle is home to some of the most picturesque beaches in the United States. With sugar-white sands, turquoise waters, and a mix of bustling tourist spots and hidden gems, there's a beach for every type of traveler. Here's a guide to some of the best beaches, including both popular and lesser-known spots, complete with lodging, dining, activities, and coordinates to help you find them.

1. Destin Beach
Coordinates: 30.3935° N, 86.4958° W

Known for its emerald waters and soft, sugar-white sand, Destin Beach is perfect for families and water enthusiasts. Fishing, paddleboarding, and dolphin tours are popular activities.

Restaurants:

The Back Porch: A classic beachfront restaurant known for its casual atmosphere and fresh seafood. Favorites include their chargrilled amberjack and seafood platters. Perfect for families, with a deck overlooking the Gulf.

Address: 1740 Scenic Hwy 98, Destin, Florida32541

Contact: (850) 837-2022

Dewey Destin's Harborside: A local staple offering fried fish baskets, shrimp, and a family-friendly vibe. Located on the harbor, it provides a taste of old Destin charm.

Address: 202 Harbor Blvd, Destin, Florida 32541

Contact: (850) 837-7575

Hotels:

<u>Beachside Inn:</u> A cozy and affordable boutique hotel just steps from the sand. It offers clean, comfortable rooms and an attached café serving fresh pastries and coffee. Bonus: free beach chairs for guests.

Address: 2931 Scenic Hwy 98, Destin, Florida 32541

Contact: (850) 650-9099

<u>Inn on Destin Harbor:</u> A charming waterfront hotel with affordable rates, offering stunning views of Destin Harbor. Guests can savor a complimentary breakfast to start their day and unwind by the serene harbor front pool, providing a perfect setting for relaxation amidst picturesque surroundings.

Address: 402 Harbor Blvd, Destin, Florida32541

Contact: (850) 837-7326

Things to Do:

Take a dolphin-watching tour.

Visit Big Kahuna's Water & Adventure Park for family fun.

2. Grayton Beach

Coordinates: 30.3313° N, 86.1619° W

Grayton Beach offers a laid-back vibe with pristine sands and dunes. The adjacent Grayton Beach State Park is ideal for hiking, fishing, and exploring natural habitats.

Restaurants:

<u>Chanticleer Eatery:</u> Known for its creative takes on comfort food, Chanticleer offers hearty sandwiches, fresh salads, and house-baked bread in a casual garden setting.

Address: 55 Clayton Ln, Santa Rosa Beach, Florida32459

Contact: (850) 213-9065

AJ's Grayton Beach: A fun, family-friendly spot with live music, Gulf-inspired dishes, and a kids' menu. Their seafood tacos and grouper sandwiches are a hit.

Address: 63 Defuniak St, Santa Rosa Beach, Florida32459

Contact: (850) 231-4102

Hotels:

The Lodge at Camp Helen State Park: A rustic and affordable accommodation surrounded by nature. The lodge features simple rooms and easy access to the beach and nearby trails.

Address: 23937 US-98, Santa Rosa Beach, Florida 32459

Contact: (850) 233-5059

Grayton Coast Rentals: A collection of quaint cottages and houses perfect for families or couples looking for a private beach experience. Rentals are fully equipped with kitchens and porches.

Contact: Available via Grayton Coast Rentals

Things to Do:

Paddleboard on Western Lake.

Shop local art at the Grayton Artist Collective.

3. Panama City Beach
Coordinates: 30.1766° N, 85.8055° W

Known for its lively atmosphere, family attractions, and 27 miles of coastline, Panama City Beach is a top destination for beachgoers.

Restaurants:

Pineapple Willy's: A beachfront institution serving up ribs, seafood baskets, and frozen cocktails. Enjoy your meal on their famous pier with ocean views.

Address: 9875 S Thomas Dr, Panama City Beach, Florida 32408

Contact: (850) 235-1225

The Shrimp Basket: A casual eatery specializing in fried shrimp, po'boys, and Southern sides. Affordable and family-friendly.

Address: 3016 Thomas Dr, Panama City Beach, Florida32408

Contact: (850) 233-1123

Hotels:

Chateau by the Sea: An old-school, budget-friendly beachfront hotel with a pool and private beach access. Rooms are basic but clean, with Gulf views.

Address: 12525 Front Beach Rd, Panama City Beach, Florida 32407

Contact: (850) 234-2174

Days Inn by Wyndham Panama City Beach: Affordable beachfront accommodations with a poolside bar and complimentary breakfast. A great choice for budget travelers.

Address: 12818 Front Beach Rd, Panama City Beach, Florida 32407

Contact: (850) 233-3333

Things to Do:

Explore Shell Island by boat or kayak.

Visit Ripley's Believe It or Not! Museum.

4. Navarre Beach

Coordinates: 30.3756° N, 86.8693° W

Navarre Beach is perfect for those seeking tranquility. Its calm waters and long pier make it a favorite for families and fishing enthusiasts.

Restaurants:

Broussard's of Navarre Beach: A casual spot with Cajun-inspired dishes and Gulf views. Don't miss their shrimp étouffée or jambalaya.

Address: 8649 Gulf Blvd, Navarre Beach, Florida 32566

Contact: (850) 396-6099

Windjammers on the Pier: A relaxed eatery offering burgers, seafood, and tropical drinks. Located right on Navarre Beach Pier, it's ideal for sunset views.

Address: 8579 Gulf Blvd, Navarre Beach, Florida 32566

Contact: (850) 710-3239

Hotels:

Navarre Beach Marine Park Cottages: Quaint cottages offer a peaceful retreat with fully equipped kitchens and private porches.

Address: 8640 Blue Heron Ct, Navarre Beach, Florida 32566

Contact: (850) 939-4411

Hampton Inn & Suites Navarre: Affordable and reliable lodging with a pool, gym, and complimentary breakfast. Located a short drive from the beach.

Address: 7710 Navarre Pkwy, Navarre, Florida 32566

Contact: (850) 939-4848

Things to Do:

Rent a bike to explore the Navarre Beach Sea Turtle Conservation Center.

Fish off the Navarre Beach Pier.

5. St. George Island (Lesser-Known)

Coordinates: 29.6592° N, 84.8802° W

St. George Island is a hidden gem on the Gulf Coast, offering 28 miles of unspoiled beaches, serene natural beauty, and a peaceful ambiance perfect for relaxation. It's part of the Forgotten Coast and is known for its laid-back charm, ideal for those seeking a quieter escape.

Restaurants:

Blue Parrot Oceanfront Café A relaxed beachfront restaurant offering fresh seafood, tropical drinks, and views of the Gulf. Their signature dishes include crab-stuffed grouper and blackened shrimp. Outdoor seating under tiki umbrellas enhances the coastal vibe.

Address: 68 W Gorrie Dr, St. George Island, Florida 32328

Contact: (850) 927-2987

Paddy's Raw Bar: A casual and fun spot for fresh oysters, craft beers, and live music. The open-air dining area creates a welcoming, island-style atmosphere. Popular menu items include steamed shrimp and fried grouper sandwiches.

Address: 240 E 3rd St, St. George Island, Florida 32328

Contact: (850) 927-2299

Hotels:

St. George Inn: A charming, budget-friendly boutique inn located near the island's main attractions. This cozy spot features simple, clean rooms with balconies offering views of the bay. Guests can enjoy the convenience of nearby restaurants and a short walk to the beach.

Address: 135 Franklin Blvd, St. George Island, Florida 32328

Contact: (850) 927-2903

Buccaneer Inn: A quaint beachfront property with affordable rooms and suites, offering direct access to the beach and a pool. The casual atmosphere and friendly staff make it a great choice for families and couples. Many rooms feature Gulf-view balconies.

Address: 160 W Gorrie Dr, St. George Island, Florida 32328

Contact: (850) 927-2585

Things to Do:

Explore St. George Island State Park: A haven for nature lovers with pristine beaches, hiking trails, and opportunities for birdwatching and kayaking.

Climb the Cape St. George Lighthouse: Learn about the island's history while enjoying panoramic views from the top of this restored lighthouse.

Fishing: The island is renowned for surf fishing and offshore charters targeting species like redfish, trout, and grouper.

Stargazing: With minimal light pollution, St. George Island is ideal for stargazing; plan a visit during a meteor shower for an unforgettable experience.

A Journey Through Time and Culture

Northwest Florida, often referred to as "The Panhandle," is more than its pristine beaches and scenic beauty. It is a treasure trove of history, shaped by centuries of cultural exchange, military significance, and artistic expression. From early Native American settlements to colonial conquests and modern architecture, the Panhandle tells a story that is anything but ordinary.

Ancient Beginnings: The Native American Legacy

Long before European explorers arrived, the Panhandle was home to the Creek, Seminole, and Apalachee tribes. The Apalachee, known for their agricultural skills, thrived in this fertile region, growing corn and beans. Evidence of their advanced culture can still be seen at **Lake Jackson Mounds State Park** near Tallahassee, where ancient earthen mounds served as ceremonial and political centers.

Trivia

Did you know that the Apalachee were among the first Native Americans to encounter Spanish explorers? Their bravery was noted by Hernando de Soto himself, who described their villages as fortified and strategically located near rivers.

Colonial Conquests: Spanish, French, and British Influence

In the 16th century, Spanish explorers such as Tristán de Luna and Hernando de Soto made their way to the Panhandle. Pensacola, established in 1559 by de Luna, is recognized as the oldest European settlement in the United States. Although a hurricane wiped out the colony, it set the stage for future Spanish, French, and British settlements.

Architecture

Colonial influences are evident in Pensacola's Seville Historic District, where Spanish-style courtyards and wrought-iron balconies mingle with British Georgian brick homes. The **T.T. Wentworth Jr. Florida State Museum**, housed in a neoclassical 1907 building, reflects this architectural blend.

The Civil War and Beyond: A Crossroads of Conflict

Northwest Florida held significant strategic value during the Civil War, with both Confederate and Union forces vying for control of the region. Its location along crucial waterways and the Gulf of Mexico made it a focal point for military operations and coastal defense throughout the conflict. Fort Pickens on Santa Rosa Island remained under Union control throughout the war and was a critical defense point. Today, visitors can explore its impressive brick arches and learn about its role in the Pensacola Harbor Defense.

Trivia

Did you know that Apache leader Geronimo was imprisoned at Fort Pickens? This surprising chapter in history draws many visitors to the fort.

Victorian Elegance and Small-Town Charm

Post-Civil War Northwest Florida saw the rise of towns like DeFuniak Springs, developed around the Chautauqua cultural movement. The town's Victorian homes, many of which are still standing, reflect an era of optimism and artistic innovation. The town even boasts one of the world's few perfectly round natural lakes.

Architecture

Victorian homes here often feature elaborate woodwork, wrap-around porches, and stained-glass windows, offering a glimpse into the late 19th century's artistic priorities.

Artistic Legacy and Folk Traditions

The Panhandle has long been a haven for artists and craftsmen. The **Quincy Art Center** showcases regional art inspired by the natural beauty of Northwest Florida. Folk traditions, such as quilt-making and storytelling, thrive in towns like Marianna and Apalachicola, where local festivals celebrate these crafts.

Trivia

Apalachicola, known for its oyster industry, also has an artistic side. The town's maritime museum houses intricate models of 19th-century boats crafted by local artisans.

A Blend of Cultures in Modern Times

Today, Northwest Florida continues to celebrate its diverse heritage. Events like the Pensacola Seafood Festival and the Scottish Highland Games in Marianna highlight the region's cultural mix. Modern architecture, such as the clean lines of the Gulf Quest National Maritime Museum, coexists with preserved historic structures, making the Panhandle a fascinating blend of old and new.

Final Thoughts

Northwest Florida's history is as varied as its landscapes, offering something for everyone—from history buffs to art lovers and architecture enthusiasts. The towns and landmarks of the region are not merely remnants of the past but are vibrant symbols of a community that honors its heritage while looking forward to the future. Whether strolling through the historic streets of Pensacola or admiring the Victorian architecture of De Funiak Springs, you're immersing yourself in a story that continues to evolve.

Historic towns to explore

1. Pensacola

- **Coordinates**: 30.4213° N, 87.2169° W
- **Overview**: Pensacola, established in 1559, holds the title of the oldest European settlement in mainland America. Its historic district reflects Spanish, French, and British influences.
- **Key Attractions**:
    - **Historic Pensacola Village**: A collection of preserved 19th-century buildings with guided tours.
    - **Fort Barrancas**: A restored fort with underground tunnels and sweeping Gulf views.
    - **Seville Square**: A public park surrounded by historic architecture.
- **Things to Do**:
    - Head to the Pensacola Lighthouse and Maritime Museum for sweeping, breathtaking views.
    - Attend events at **Seville Quarter**, a lively hub in restored historic buildings.

2. Apalachicola

- **Coordinates**: 29.7258° N, 84.9830° W
- **Overview**: This charming riverside town is renowned for its historic architecture and world-class oysters.
- **Key Attractions**:
    - **Orman House Historic State Park**: Tour a stately home with artifacts from the 19th century.
    - **Apalachicola Maritime Museum**: Dive into the town's seafaring heritage.
    - **Chestnut Street Cemetery**: A historic burial site dating back to 1831.
- **Things to Do**:
    - Sample fresh seafood at local restaurants along the riverfront.

- Explore boutique shops and art galleries in the charming downtown area.

3. DeFuniak Springs (Lesser-Known)

- **Coordinates**: 30.7216° N, 86.1158° W
- **Overview**: Known for its Victorian charm, this town boasts one of only two perfectly circular natural lakes in the world.
- **Key Attractions**:
    - **Walton-DeFuniak Library**: Established in 1887, it's Florida's oldest library still in use.
    - **Chautauqua Hall of Brotherhood**: A historic auditorium hosting cultural events.
    - **Circle Drive**: A scenic road surrounded by Victorian-era homes.
- **Things to Do**:
    - Attend the **Florida Chautauqua Assembly**, a unique educational event.
    - Picnic by **Lake DeFuniak**, enjoying its serene surroundings.

4. Marianna (Lesser-Known)

- **Coordinates**: 30.7749° N, 85.2269° W
- **Overview**: Known as the "City of Southern Charm," Marianna boasts a mix of natural beauty and Civil War history.
- **Key Attractions**:
    - **Florida Caverns State Park**: The only air-filled caves in Florida open to the public.
    - **The Battle of Marianna Monument**: A tribute to a Civil War skirmish.
    - **Downtown Historic District**: Explore quaint streets lined with shops and historic buildings.
- **Things to Do**:
    - Hike or bike the **Chipola River Greenway**.

- Kayak or paddle along the crystal-clear waters of the Chipola River.

Three-Day Itinerary for Northwest Florida: The Panhandle

Experience a thoughtfully planned vacation highlighting history, nature, and the region's breathtaking beauty without breaking the bank. This itinerary balances visits to historic sites, scenic beaches, and serene outdoor locations, while recommending affordable accommodations, dining options, and memorable sunset spots.

Day 1: History and Charm in Pensacola

<u>Morning</u>

Breakfast at The Ruby Slipper Café

509 S Palafox St, Pensacola, Florida 32502

+1 (850) 792-4834

Enjoy a Southern-style breakfast with items like Eggs Benedict or sweet pancakes. Budget-friendly and centrally located.

Historic Pensacola Village

330 S Jefferson St, Pensacola, Florida 32502

+1 (850) 595-5985

Explore this collection of historic homes and museums, including the T.T. Wentworth Museum and the Old Christ Church. Admission: ~$10 for a full day pass.

<u>Afternoon</u>

Lunch at Hub Stacey's Downtown

312 E Government St, Pensacola, Florida 32502

+1 (850) 469-1001

Affordable deli sandwiches and casual dining in a cozy atmosphere. Try the turkey pesto panini.

Fort Pickens

Gulf Islands National Seashore, Pensacola Beach, Florida 32561

Coordinates: [30.3274° N, 87.2908° W]

Explore the historic Civil War-era fort and learn about its role in military history. Entry fee: $25 per vehicle (valid for a week).

Evening

Dinner at The Fish House

600 S Barracks St, Pensacola, Florida 32502

+1 (850) 470-0003

Affordable seafood with a beautiful view of the waterfront. Try the grits à ya ya or the fresh catch of the day.

Stay at Sole Inn and Suites

200 N Palafox St, Pensacola, Florida 32502

+1 (850) 470-9298

A budget-friendly boutique hotel situated in downtown Pensacola. The rooms offer a cozy atmosphere, and guests can enjoy a complimentary breakfast to start their day.

Day 2: Beaches and Coastal Adventures

Morning

Breakfast at Café Single Fin

731 Pensacola Beach Blvd, Gulf Breeze, Florida 32561

+1 (850) 677-8874

Chill vibe with great coffee and breakfast burritos. Perfect for a beach day starter.

Navarre Beach

Navarre Beach, Florida 32566

Coordinates: [30.3783° N, 86.8658° W]

Known as "Florida's Most Relaxing Place," enjoy sugar-white sands and clear waters. Activities include snorkeling or renting paddleboards from local vendors.

Afternoon

Lunch at Windjammers on the Pier

8579 Gulf Blvd, Navarre Beach, Florida 32566

+1 (850) 710-3239

Affordable, beachy food like fish tacos and burgers, with stunning views of the Gulf.

Relax at Blackwater River State Forest

11650 Munson Hwy, Milton, Florida 32570

Coordinates: [30.7277° N, 86.8672° W]

A scenic escape into nature. Rent a kayak or enjoy an easy hiking trail.

Evening

Sunset at Gulf Islands National Seashore

Fort Pickens Rd, Pensacola Beach, Florida 32561

Enjoy a quiet, romantic sunset along the shore. Don't forget to bring your camera!

Dinner at Peg Leg Pete's

1010 Fort Pickens Rd, Pensacola Beach, Florida 32561

+1 (850) 932-4139

Known for fresh seafood, live music, and a casual atmosphere. Try their oysters or seafood platter.

Stay at Hampton Inn & Suites Navarre

7710 Navarre Pkwy, Navarre, Florida 32566

+1 (850) 939-4848

Affordable and conveniently located near the beach with free breakfast and a pool.

Day 3: Apalachicola and St. George Island

Morning

Breakfast at The Café con Leche

234 Water St, Apalachicola, Florida 32320

+1 (850) 653-2233

Small-town charm with great coffee and homemade pastries.

Explore Apalachicola

Coordinates: [29.7258° N, 84.9833° W]

Stroll through the charming streets, visit the Apalachicola Maritime Museum, and admire the historic homes with their antebellum architecture.

Afternoon

Lunch at The Owl Café

15 Avenue D, Apalachicola, Florida 32320

+1 (850) 653-9888

Affordable fine dining with Southern flavors. Try the fried green tomatoes or grouper sandwich.

St. George Island State Park

1900 E Gulf Beach Dr, St. George Island, Florida 32328

Coordinates: [29.7324° N, 84.8034° W]

A tranquil beach with opportunities for birdwatching, shelling, and hiking. Entry fee: $6 per vehicle.

Evening

Dinner at Paddy's Raw Bar

240 E 3rd St, St. George Island, Florida 32328

+1 (850) 927-2299

Casual seafood spot known for oysters and cold beer. Family-friendly and affordable.

Stay at St. George Inn

135 Franklin Blvd, St. George Island, Florida 32328

+1 (850) 927-2903

Charming inn with cozy, nautical-themed rooms and friendly service. Ideal for exploring the island.

NORTHEAST FLORIDA

A Region of Rich History and Unique Beauty

Northeast Florida, often referred to as Florida's "First Coast," boasts a blend of historic significance, natural beauty, and vibrant culture. Stretching from the historic city of St. Augustine to the charming communities of Amelia Island and Jacksonville, this region is a treasure trove for travelers seeking a mix of fascinating history, outdoor adventures, and serene coastal escapes.

Coastal Beauty and Outdoor Fun

Northeast Florida is defined by its scenic Atlantic coastline, offering a mix of tranquil beaches, salt marshes, and barrier islands. This area is ideal for sunbathing, kayaking, fishing, or exploring wildlife refuges. The region's ecosystems, including the Guana Tolomato Matanzas Reserve, highlight its ecological diversity.

Historical Richness

Northeast Florida, often referred to as the "cradle of European colonization" in America, boasts a rich history that traces back to 1565. It was in St. Augustine, the oldest continuously inhabited European settlement in the United States, that this era began. From the Spanish colonial period to the Gilded Age, the area's layered history is visible in its well-preserved architecture and landmarks.

Beyond the historical landmarks, towns like Fernandina Beach and Jacksonville provide a mix of modern cultural offerings, art galleries, and unique dining experiences.

Historical Notes and Fascinating Stories

St. Augustine and Its Founding

Established in 1565 by Spanish admiral Pedro Menéndez de Avilés, St. Augustine is steeped in history. The city endured battles, hurricanes, and colonial rivalries, leaving behind landmarks like the Castillo de San Marcos, a 17th-century fortress made of coquina stone, and the Cathedral Basilica of St. Augustine, the oldest parish in the U.S.

Historical Trivia: During Prohibition, the waterways around St. Augustine were hotbeds for rum-running, with locals smuggling alcohol from the Caribbean.

Amelia Island's Pirate Past

Known as the "Isle of Eight Flags," Amelia Island is the only place in the U.S. to have been ruled by eight different nations. Its pirate lore and role in the shrimping industry give it a distinctive charm.

Architectural Note: The historic district of Fernandina Beach on Amelia Island showcases Victorian-era buildings, many of which were built during the late 1800s shrimping boom.

Jacksonville's Modern Renaissance

Jacksonville played a significant role during the Civil War as a strategic port for both Union and Confederate forces. Today, it blends modern skyscrapers with historic districts like Riverside and Avondale, where you'll find early 20th-century bungalow-style homes.

Must-see tourist attractions

1. Castillo de San Marcos, St. Augustine

Coordinates: [29.8978° N, 81.3123° W]

Why Visit: This 17th-century fort is the oldest masonry structure in the U.S., showcasing Spanish military engineering and offering stunning views of Matanzas Bay.

Interesting Feature: Watch historical reenactments, including cannon firings, that bring its past to life.

2. Amelia Island State Park

Coordinates: [30.5248° N, 81.4594° W]

Why Visit: Known for its unspoiled beaches and pristine dunes, this park is perfect for horseback riding along the shoreline.

Lesser-Known Fact: It's a great spot for shelling and spotting gopher tortoises.

3. Fort Clinch State Park, Amelia Island

Coordinates: [30.6784° N, 81.4333° W]

Why Visit: A beautifully preserved 19th-century fort surrounded by scenic trails and picnic areas.

Interesting Trivia: The fort was never used in battle, but soldiers occupied it during the Civil War, Spanish-American War, and World War II.

4. Jacksonville's Riverside and Avondale Historic Districts

Coordinates: [30.3087° N, 81.6885° W]

Why Visit: Stroll along oak-lined streets to admire early 20th-century homes and enjoy eclectic shopping and dining options.

Architectural Note: The area is known for its mix of bungalow and prairie-style homes, reflecting the Arts and Crafts movement.

5. Guana Tolomato Matanzas National Estuarine Research Reserve

Coordinates: [30.0518° N, 81.3272° W]

Why Visit: Explore this tranquil reserve with hiking trails, birdwatching, and kayaking opportunities.

Lesser-Known Fact: It's a hotspot for spotting dolphins and manatees.

6. Kingsley Plantation, Jacksonville

Coordinates: [30.4405° N, 81.4398° W]

Why Visit: Step back in time to learn about plantation life in the 19th century.

Interesting Trivia: Zephaniah Kingsley, the plantation owner, was married to Anna, an enslaved woman who became a free landowner after gaining her freedom.

7. Big Talbot Island State Park

Coordinates: [30.4932° N, 81.4444° W]

Why Visit: A serene park known for Boneyard Beach, where fallen trees create a dramatic natural sculpture garden.

Interesting Trivia: It's a favorite spot for photographers, especially at sunrise.

8. Lightner Museum, St. Augustine

Coordinates: [29.8948° N, 81.3133° W]

Why Visit: Located in the former Alcazar Hotel, this museum showcases an eclectic collection of 19th-century artifacts, from Tiffany glass to shrunken heads.

Architectural Note: The building is a masterpiece of Spanish Renaissance Revival style, designed by Carrère and Hastings in 1888.

A Perfect Day in St. Augustine

A Smart, Relaxed Itinerary

St. Augustine, the oldest continuously inhabited European-established city in the U.S., is a treasure trove of history, art, and culture. With its cobblestone streets, centuries-old landmarks, and artistic charm, it's a must-visit destination. Below is a one-day itinerary that balances historical exploration, artistic indulgence, great local dining, and relaxing strolls.

Morning: Dive Into History

Start at Castillo de San Marcos

- **Address**: 1 S Castillo Dr - St. Augustine - FL 32084
- **Contact**: +1 (904) 829-6506
- **Hours**: 9:00 AM - 5:00 PM
- **Entry Fee**: $15 for adults; free for children under 16. Begin your day at this iconic 17th-century Spanish fortress. Built from coquina stone, the fort showcases impressive engineering and a fascinating history. Explore its walls, learn about the battles fought here, and enjoy panoramic views of Matanzas Bay. Historical reenactments and cannon firings often take place in the morning.

Breakfast at The Bunnery Bakery & Café

- **Address**: 121 St. George St, St. Augustine, Florida 32084
- **Contact**: +1 (904) 829-6166
- **Why Go**: This cozy spot is perfect for a quick and hearty breakfast. Try their freshly baked pastries, breakfast sandwiches, or a steaming cup of coffee before heading to your next stop.

Visit the Colonial Quarter

- **Address**: 33 St. George St, St. Augustine, Florida 32084
- **Contact**: +1 (888) 991-0933
- **Hours**: 10:00 AM - 6:00 PM
  Stroll through the living history museum that recreates life in St. Augustine during the Spanish and British colonial periods. Watch blacksmithing demonstrations, climb a reconstructed watchtower, and immerse yourself in the daily life of 16th-18th century settlers.

Midday: Art and Local Dining

Lunch at The Floridian

- **Address**: 72 Spanish St, St. Augustine, Florida 32084
- **Contact**: +1 (904) 829-0655
- **Why Go**: Located just steps from the Colonial Quarter, this laid-back eatery serves Southern-inspired dishes with a creative twist. Try their shrimp and grits or the fried green tomato sandwich for a taste of the region. Vegetarian options abound!

A Day Immersed in Jacksonville's Vibrant Arts Scene

Jacksonville, the largest city in Florida by area, boasts a thriving arts scene that reflects its rich history, cultural diversity, and creative spirit. Whether you're exploring colorful murals, intimate galleries, or celebrated performance venues, the city offers something for every art enthusiast. Below is a thoughtfully planned one-day itinerary designed to showcase Jacksonville's creative soul.

<u>Morning: Start with Art and History</u>

Cummer Museum of Art & Gardens

Address: 829 Riverside Ave, Jacksonville, Florida 32204

Contact: +1 (904) 356-6857

Hours: 11:00 AM - 4:00 PM (Check for extended hours or special events.)

Entry Fee: $10 for adults, $6 for seniors, free for children under 6.

Begin your day at Jacksonville's premier art museum. The Cummer Museum houses an impressive collection of over 5,000 works, spanning from ancient artifacts to 21st-century pieces. Highlights include its European and American art collections and the stunning riverside gardens, offering a serene blend of culture and natural beauty.

Breakfast Nearby: Cool Moose Café

Address: 2708 Park St, Jacksonville, Florida 32205

Contact: +1 (904) 381-4242

Why Go: This quirky café in Riverside serves hearty breakfasts with a touch of creativity. Try their signature stuffed French toast or veggie-loaded omelets, paired with fresh-brewed coffee. The relaxed vibe is perfect to fuel your day of art exploration.

Late Morning: Explore Local Creativity

Riverside Arts Market (Saturdays Only)

Address: 715 Riverside Ave, Jacksonville, Florida 32204

Contact: +1 (904) 389-2449

Hours: 10:00 AM - 3:00 PM (Saturday only)

This bustling open-air market, located under the Fuller Warren Bridge, showcases local artists, artisans, and performers. Browse handcrafted jewelry, unique paintings, and sculptures while enjoying live music and delicious snacks from food vendors.

Lunch: A Local Favorite

Lunch at Maple Street Biscuit Company

Address: 2004 San Marco Blvd - Jacksonville - FL 32207

Contact: +1 (904) 398-1004

Why Visit: Maple Street is renowned for its Southern-inspired biscuits with a creative twist, offering a menu filled with delicious comfort food. One must-try dish is the "Squawking Goat," a flavorful biscuit topped with fried chicken, goat cheese, and a touch of pepper jelly. This delightful dish is served in the vibrant San Marco area, making it an ideal stop before continuing on to your next adventure.

Afternoon: Dive Into Public Art and Galleries

Explore the Downtown Jacksonville Art Walk (First Wednesday Only)

Address: Various locations in Downtown Jacksonville

Contact: +1 (904) 634-0303

This self-guided art walk features an array of galleries, studios, and pop-up exhibits. If your visit doesn't coincide with the Art Walk, you can still explore downtown murals, including the iconic "Jax Mural" by Shaun Thurston (📍 108 E Forsyth St).

MOCA Jacksonville (Museum of Contemporary Art)

Address: 333 N Laura St, Jacksonville, Florida 32202

Contact: +1 (904) 366-6911

Hours: 11:00 AM - 5:00 PM

Entry Fee: $8 for adults, $5 for children.

MOCA Jacksonville features dynamic contemporary exhibitions that rotate regularly, alongside permanent works. Interactive programs often engage visitors, making it a favorite spot for families and art aficionados alike.

Evening: Relaxation and Performance Arts

Dinner at Taverna

Address: 1986 San Marco Blvd – Jacksonville - FL 32207

Contact: +1 (904) 398-3005

Why Go: Located in the heart of San Marco, Taverna specializes in fresh, handmade pasta and wood-fired pizzas. The rustic yet refined ambiance pairs perfectly with dishes like their signature fettuccine or margherita pizza.

Cap Off the Day at the Florida Theatre

Address: 128 E Forsyth St, Jacksonville, Florida 32202

Contact: +1 (904) 355-5661

A Day Exploring Amelia Island's Charming Coastal Retreats

Amelia Island, one of Florida's most enchanting destinations, offers a blend of natural beauty, fascinating history, and a laid-back coastal vibe. Known for its pristine beaches, elegant Victorian-era architecture, and warm southern charm, this barrier island is the perfect escape for those seeking tranquility and timeless allure. Below is a one-day itinerary that highlights the best of Amelia Island's scenic and cultural treasures.

Morning: Start with History and Natural Beauty

Historic Downtown Fernandina Beach

Address: Centre St, Fernandina Beach, Florida 32034

Why Go: Begin your day strolling through the heart of Amelia Island's history. Fernandina Beach is home to 50 blocks of preserved Victorian architecture. Explore the quaint streets lined with boutique shops, art galleries, and historic landmarks like the Palace Saloon—Florida's oldest bar.

Trivia: Fernandina Beach has the distinction of being the only U.S. city to have flown eight different national flags, a reflection of its diverse history.

Breakfast Nearby: Amelia Island Coffee

Address: 207 Centre St, Fernandina Beach, Florida 32034

Contact: +1 (904) 321-2111

Why Go: This cozy café serves up fresh coffee, pastries, and breakfast sandwiches. Try their signature "Island Delight Latte" with a croissant for a quick, satisfying start to your day.

Late Morning: Explore the Coastline

Fort Clinch State Park

Address: 2601 Atlantic Ave, Fernandina Beach, Florida 32034

Contact: +1 (904) 277-7274

Why Go: Step back in time with a visit to Fort Clinch, a beautifully preserved Civil War-era fort. Visitors can explore the fort's brick bastions, cannons, and historical exhibits while enjoying stunning views of Cumberland Sound. The surrounding park offers miles of walking trails, beachcombing, and wildlife spotting.

Admission: $6 per vehicle, $2.50 for fort access.

Lunch: A Relaxing Coastal Spot

Timoti's Seafood Shak

Address: 21 N 3rd St, Fernandina Beach, Florida 32034

Contact: +1 (904) 310-6550

Why Go: This casual eatery is a favorite for fresh, sustainable seafood. Enjoy their famous shrimp basket, fish tacos, or a lobster roll in their outdoor seating area, shaded by a charming pergola.

Afternoon: Coastal Relaxation

Main Beach Park

Address: 32 N Fletcher Ave, Fernandina Beach, Florida 32034

Why Go: Spend the afternoon soaking up the sun at Main Beach Park, one of Amelia Island's most popular spots. With soft sand, calm waters, and nearby amenities like volleyball courts and picnic areas, it's perfect for families and solo travelers alike. For a quieter experience, head slightly north to Peters Point Beachfront Park (4600 Peters Point Rd).

Activity Option: Book a dolphin-watching or eco-tour cruise with Amelia River Cruises (1 N Front St). These guided excursions offer incredible opportunities to spot wildlife, including dolphins, manatees, and seabirds.

Evening: Sunset and Dinner

Sunset at Amelia Island Lighthouse

Address: 215 O'Hagan Ln, Fernandina Beach, Florida 32034

Why Go: Cap off your day with a visit to Florida's oldest lighthouse. Although the lighthouse isn't open to the public, the grounds offer a picturesque setting for viewing the sunset over Egans Creek marsh.

Dinner: Arte Pizza

Address: 109 N 3rd St, Fernandina Beach, Florida 32034

Contact: +1 (904) 277-1515

Why Go: This casual Italian spot is beloved for its wood-fired pizzas, pasta, and fresh salads. Try the "Amelia Supreme" pizza with local shrimp or their handmade lasagna. The cozy, family-friendly atmosphere makes it a great way to unwind after a full day.

Hidden Gem Itinerary for Northeast Florida

Ideal for Nature Enthusiasts and Horseback Riders

For travelers seeking a quieter, off-the-beaten-path adventure in Northeast Florida, this itinerary focuses on stunning natural landscapes, secluded beaches, and unique horseback riding experiences. These locations are beloved by locals and provide an alternative escape, perfect for those looking to avoid heavily trafficked tourist spots like Amelia Island, Jacksonville, or St. Augustine.

Day 1: Exploring Big Talbot Island State Park

Morning: Hike Through Big Talbot Island

Address: 12157 Heckscher Dr, Jacksonville, Florida 32226

Why Visit: This unique park is a sanctuary for nature lovers, with its famous Boneyard Beach, where fallen trees have weathered into stunning sculptures along the shore. The park features hiking trails like Blackrock Trail, which leads to a picturesque, rocky shoreline. Birdwatchers can spot herons, egrets, and ospreys.

Coordinates: 30.4925° N, 81.4580° W

Lunch: Sandollar Restaurant

Address: 9716 Heckscher Dr, Jacksonville, Florida 32226

Contact: +1 (904) 251-2449

Why Eat Here: Located near the park, this casual waterfront spot serves fresh seafood with a view of the St. Johns River. Their fried shrimp and crab cakes are local favorites, paired with a refreshing sweet tea.

Afternoon: Kayaking or Paddleboarding

Activity: Rent a kayak or paddleboard from Kayak Amelia (13030 Heckscher Dr, Jacksonville, Florida 32226) and explore the calm waters of Simpson Creek. This is a serene way to immerse yourself in the island's ecosystem, paddling past salt marshes and spotting dolphins and manatees.

Dinner: Palms Fish Camp Restaurant

Address: 6359 Heckscher Dr, Jacksonville, Florida 32226

Contact: +1 (904) 240-1672

Why Eat Here: A favorite among locals, this riverside eatery offers affordable, fresh seafood and Southern classics. Their blackened grouper and hush puppies are a must-try, and the sunset views are unbeatable.

Day 2: Beachfront Horseback Riding and Secluded Nature Trails

Morning: Horseback Riding on Ponte Vedra Beach

Activity: Book a horseback riding experience with Kelly Seahorse Ranch (7500 Sawgrass Village Cir, Ponte Vedra Beach, Florida 32082). Their guided horseback rides along the pristine shores of Guana Tolomato Matanzas National Estuarine Research Reserve provide an unmatched sense of tranquility.

Why go: It's a unique and enchanting way to experience Florida's coastline. The reserve, full of diverse wildlife, offers a peaceful atmosphere, making it a hidden gem for horseback riders.

Lunch: Cap's on the Water

Address: 4325 Myrtle St, St. Augustine, Florida 32084

Contact: +1 (904) 824-8794

Why Eat Here: Nestled along the Intracoastal Waterway, this charming restaurant offers a blend of seafood and Southern favorites. Their shrimp and grits and fresh oysters are particularly delicious. Enjoy dining under their oak-shaded deck with beautiful water views.

Afternoon: Guana Tolomato Matanzas Reserve Trails

Address: 505 Guana River Rd, Ponte Vedra Beach, Florida 32082

Why Visit: Hike the Ravine Loop Trail, which winds through lush coastal forests and offers glimpses of the marshlands. For a unique experience, visit the Environmental Education Center to learn about the area's ecosystems and history.

Coordinates: 30.0920° N, 81.3278° W

Dinner: Valley Smoke BBQ

Address: 11 S Roscoe Blvd, Ponte Vedra Beach, Florida 32082

Contact: +1 (904) 834-3473

Why Eat Here: This unpretentious barbecue joint combines traditional smoked meats with a modern twist. Their brisket tacos and pulled pork sandwiches are crowd-pleasers, and their riverside patio is perfect for relaxing.

Day 3: Exploring Faver-Dykes State Park and Flagler Beach

Morning: Canoeing at Faver-Dykes State Park

Address: 1000 Faver Dykes Rd, St. Augustine, Florida 32086

Contact: +1 (386) 446-6783

Why Visit: Escape the crowds with a visit to this peaceful park. Rent a canoe or kayak to explore the Pellicer Creek, a designated State Canoe Trail. Keep an eye out for otters, alligators, and bald eagles as you paddle through the lush surroundings.

Coordinates: 29.6811° N, 81.2457° W

Lunch: JT's Seafood Shack

Address: 5224 N Oceanshore Blvd, Palm Coast, Florida 32137

Contact: +1 (386) 446-4337

Why Eat Here: This rustic, family-run restaurant is known for its laid-back vibe and tasty seafood dishes. Try their shrimp po' boy or fish tacos, and pair it with a local craft beer.

Afternoon: Relax at Washington Oaks Gardens State Park

Address: 6400 N Oceanshore Blvd, Palm Coast, Florida 32137

Contact: +1 (386) 446-6783

Why Visit: Known for its formal gardens and unique coquina rock formations along the shoreline, this park offers stunning photo opportunities. Wander through the rose gardens, shaded by centuries-old oaks, or explore the peaceful trails.

Coordinates: 29.6276° N, 81.2112° W

Dinner: Turtle Shack Café

Address: 2123 N Ocean Shore Blvd, Flagler Beach, Florida c32136

Contact: +1 (386) 693-4851

Why Eat Here: A local favorite, this unassuming eatery serves up hearty burgers, seafood, and tropical-inspired dishes. Their blackened mahi-mahi is a standout, and the casual beachside setting is the perfect way to wrap up your day.

CENTRAL FLORIDA

History, Art, Architecture, and Highlights

Central Florida is a dynamic and diverse region that blends natural beauty, cultural richness, and a fascinating history. Known worldwide as a hub for entertainment and tourism, it also boasts a legacy of historical landmarks, artistic treasures, and architectural marvels that reveal a deeper side of the area beyond theme parks.

A Brief Historical Overview

Central Florida's history stretches back thousands of years, originally home to the Timucua people, who thrived here for centuries before European settlers arrived in the 16th century. Spanish explorers, including Juan Ponce de León, brought profound changes to the region in their search for riches and the mythical Fountain of Youth. By the 19th century, the area saw waves of settlers drawn by Florida's abundant resources, fertile soil, and strategic location.

During the late 1800s, Central Florida became a hub for citrus farming, earning the nickname **"The Citrus Capital of the World."** The railroads, introduced by tycoons like Henry B. Plant, facilitated economic growth and spurred the development of cities like Orlando, Winter Park, and Kissimmee.

In the 20th century, the introduction of Walt Disney World in 1971 revolutionized Central Florida, transforming the region into a global tourism powerhouse. But alongside its entertainment legacy, the area retains reminders of its historical and artistic roots.

Architectural and Artistic Heritage

Central Florida's architectural styles reflect its history, ranging from Spanish Colonial Revival to Victorian, Mediterranean Revival, and Mid-Century Modern. The influence of early Spanish explorers and settlers is evident in the Mission-style churches and historic landmarks scattered throughout the area. Later, Winter Park and Orlando embraced the Victorian and Mediterranean Revival movements, resulting in neighborhoods and structures that exude charm.

Artists have long been inspired by Central Florida's lush landscapes, and you'll find works in museums and public spaces that celebrate Florida's natural beauty. Institutions like the Charles Hosmer Morse Museum of American Art house collections that include stained glass, paintings, and decorative arts, showcasing the region's contribution to American art history.

Special Features of Central Florida

Central Florida is best known for its entertainment meccas like Walt Disney World, Universal Studios, and SeaWorld. However, the region also offers serene natural landscapes, including crystal-clear springs, extensive state parks, and lakes perfect for outdoor enthusiasts.

The area's cultural diversity has enriched its food, art, and traditions, making it an exciting destination for those who appreciate a mix of old and new.

Interesting Places to Visit

Here is a list of notable destinations in Central Florida, spanning history, art, nature, and relaxation:

1. **Charles Hosmer Morse Museum of American Art**
    - **Location**: 445 N Park Ave -Winter Park- Florida 32789
    - **Coordinates**: 28.5987° N, 81.3514° W
    - **Why Visit**: Home to the world's most extensive collection of Louis Comfort Tiffany's works, including stunning stained glass windows, jewelry, and lamps.
2. **Leu Gardens**
    - **Location**: 1920 N Forest Ave – Orlando - Florida 32803
    - **Coordinates**: 28.5630° N, 81.3643° W
    - **Why Visit**: A 50-acre botanical oasis featuring tropical plants, butterfly gardens, and beautiful sculptures.
3. **Lake Eola Park**
    - **Location**: 512 E Washington St – Orlando - Florida 32801
    - **Coordinates**: 28.5434° N, 81.3697° W
    - **Why Visit**: Iconic for its swan boats and scenic lakefront, this park is a beloved urban retreat.
4. **Bok Tower Gardens**
    - **Location**: 1151 Tower Blvd - Lake Wales - Florida 33853
    - **Coordinates**: 27.9377° N, 81.5754° W
    - **Why Visit**: This historic landmark features a stunning Carillon tower, lush gardens, and peaceful trails.
5. **De Leon Springs State Park**
    - **Location**: 601 Ponce de Leon Blvd - De Leon Springs - Florida 32130
    - **Coordinates**: 29.1235° N, 81.3511° W

- Why Visit: Famous for its natural springs and the charming Old Spanish Sugar Mill, where you can make your pancakes.

6. **Mount Dora**
    - **Coordinates**: 28.8028° N, 81.6444° W
    - **Why Visit**: Known as the "New England of the South," this quaint town is filled with antique shops, art galleries, and lakeside views.

7. **Wekiwa Springs State Park**
    - **Location**: 1800 Wekiwa Cir, Apopka, Florida 32712
    - **Coordinates**: 28.7118° N, 81.4631° W
    - **Why Visit**: Perfect for kayaking, swimming, or picnicking, this park offers a refreshing escape into nature.

8. **Kissimmee Historic District**
    - **Coordinates**: 28.2919° N, 81.4075° W
    - **Why Visit**: Explore the historic architecture and local shops in this charming downtown area.

9. **The Mennello Museum of American Art**
    - **Location**: 900 E Princeton St - Orlando - Florida 32803
    - **Coordinates**: 28.5725° N, 81.3707° W
    - **Why Visit**: A hidden gem showcasing American folk art and outdoor sculptures.

Orlando: Best Theme Park Experience

Orlando is known as the Theme Park Capital of the World, with a variety of iconic parks catering to all kinds of visitors. Here's a list of the major theme parks in Orlando:

1. Walt Disney World Resort

Magic Kingdom: Famous for Cinderella Castle, classic rides like Pirates of the Caribbean, and fireworks over the castle.

Epcot: Celebrates technology and international culture, featuring the World Showcase and futuristic attractions like Spaceship Earth.

Disney's Hollywood Studios: Themed around movies and entertainment, with highlights like Star Wars: Galaxy's Edge and the Tower of Terror.

Disney's Animal Kingdom: Combines a zoo with rides and attractions like Pandora – The World of Avatar.

Blizzard Beach & Typhoon Lagoon: Disney's water parks with unique themes and attractions.

Location: Lake Buena Vista, Florida32830

Website: disneyworld.disney.go.com

2. Universal Orlando Resort

Universal Studios Florida: A working studio and park featuring movie-themed rides like Harry Potter and the Escape from Gringotts.

Islands of Adventure: Known for its immersive areas like the Wizarding World of Islands of Adventure is renowned for its highly immersive themed zones, such as The Wizarding World of Harry Potter-Hogsmeade and Marvel Super Hero Island. These areas transport visitors into beloved fictional worlds, offering exhilarating rides, themed dining experiences, and interactive attractions that bring these iconic stories to life.

Marvel Super Hero Island and Harry Potter Hogsmeade.

Volcano Bay: A tropical-themed water park with slides and wave pools.

Location: 6000 Universal Blvd, Orlando, Florida 32819

Website: universalorlando.com

3. SeaWorld Orlando

Offers marine life exhibits, thrilling coasters like Mako, and live animal shows. It also includes:

Aquatica: A water park with slides and wave pools.

Discovery Cove: An all-inclusive park where visitors can swim with dolphins and snorkel in tropical lagoons.

Location: 7007 Sea World Dr, Orlando, Florida 32821

Website: seaworld.com/orlando

4. LEGOLAND Florida Resort (Located in nearby Winter Haven)

Tailored for families with younger children, featuring LEGO-themed attractions, water parks, and interactive rides.

Location: 1 LEGOLAND Way, Winter Haven, Florida 33884

Website: legoland.com/florida

5. ICON Park

While not a traditional theme park, ICON Park is an entertainment hub with the Wheel at ICON Park, Madame Tussauds Orlando, and SEA LIFE Aquarium.

Location: 8375 International Dr, Orlando, Florida32819

Website: iconparkorlando.com

6. Gatorland

A unique park that combines nature and adventure, offering up-close encounters with alligators, a zipline over the swamp, and animal shows.

Location: 14501 S Orange Blossom Trail, Orlando, Florida32837

Website: gatorland.com

Orlando's best authentic experiences

For those seeking a more authentic and immersive experience, Orlando and its surroundings have plenty of unique offerings. Here's a guide to Orlando's best authentic experiences that allow you to dive into its culture, history, and natural beauty.

1. Explore Orlando's Local Neighborhoods

Winter Park

- **What Makes It Special**: A historic district just outside downtown Orlando, Winter Park is known for its cobblestone streets, charming boutiques, and tree-lined avenues. Founded in the late 19th century as a winter retreat, it features beautiful Mediterranean Revival architecture.
- **Must-Do Activities**:
    - Stroll along Park Avenue, with its mix of local shops, galleries, and restaurants.
    - Visit the **Charles Hosmer Morse Museum of American Art** (445 N Park Ave; Coordinates: 28.5983, -81.3517), which houses the world's largest collection of Tiffany glass.
    - Enjoy a **Scenic Boat Tour** (312 E Morse Blvd), which glides through the region's interconnected lakes and past stunning waterfront homes.

Mills 50 District

- **What Makes It Special**: This area offers a taste of Orlando's vibrant diversity, with a strong focus on Asian culture. From street art to delicious food, it's a creative hub.
- **Must-Do Activities**:
    - Sample authentic Vietnamese cuisine at **Hawkers Asian Street Fare** (1103 N Mills Ave).

- Explore local murals and independent shops like **The Lovely Boutique Market** (2906 Corrine Dr).

2. Visit Leu Gardens

- **Why Go**: A lush, 50-acre botanical garden in the heart of Orlando, **Harry P. Leu Gardens** (1920 N Forest Ave; Coordinates: 28.5647, -81.3656) offers a peaceful escape from the city's hustle.
- **Highlights**: Stroll through the rose garden, butterfly garden, and camellia collection. Don't miss the Leu House Museum, a restored turn-of-the-century home showcasing Florida's early history.

3. Paddle Through Shingle Creek

- **What Makes It Unique**: Known as the "Headwaters of the Everglades," **Shingle Creek** offers a chance to kayak or paddleboard through pristine waterways.
- **Best Spot to Start**: **Shingle Creek Regional Park** (4266 W Vine St, Kissimmee; Coordinates: 28.3043, -81.4324).
- **What to Expect**: Paddle through lush cypress forests and spot native wildlife like otters, turtles, and herons.

4. Discover Orlando's History at the Wells'Built Museum

- **What Makes It Special**: Once a hotel for African-American travelers during segregation, the **Wells'Built Museum of African American History and Culture** (511 W South St; Coordinates: 28.5355, -81.3869) showcases the history of Orlando's Black community.
- **Highlights**: Exhibits include artifacts, photographs, and memorabilia from the Civil Rights Movement and beyond.

5. Foodie Adventures in Orlando

East End Market

- **What Makes It Unique**: This indoor market (3201 Corrine Dr; Coordinates: 28.5658, -81.3462) is a haven for food lovers, offering locally sourced produce, artisanal food, and handcrafted goods.
- **Must-Try Vendors**:
    - **Gideon's Bakehouse** for its famous half-pound cookies.
    - **Domu** for creative Asian-inspired dishes and craft cocktails.

The Ravenous Pig

- **What Makes It Special**: A modern gastropub in Winter Park (565 W Fairbanks Ave; Coordinates: 28.5922, -81.3557) that focuses on locally sourced ingredients.
- **Must-Try Dishes**: Their smoked brisket and handcrafted beers are crowd favorites.

6. Catch a Sunset at Lake Eola

- **Why It's Worth It**: Located in downtown Orlando, **Lake Eola Park** (512 E Washington St; Coordinates: 28.5434, -81.3705) is an iconic spot for a leisurely evening.
- **Activities**: Rent a swan paddle boat, enjoy the park's sculpture installations, or grab a coffee at **Eola Wine Company** nearby.

7. Explore the Ocala National Forest

- **What Makes It Special**: Just a short drive from Orlando, the **Ocala National Forest** (Coordinates: 29.1713, -81.8110) is perfect for outdoor enthusiasts. It offers hiking

opportunities for hiking, swimming in crystal-clear springs, and even stargazing.
- **Must-See Springs**: Visit **Juniper Springs** (26701 FL-40, Silver Springs) for its turquoise waters and shaded trails.

8. Authentic Nightlife at Ivanhoe Village

- **What Makes It Unique**: This bohemian neighborhood offers a mix of craft breweries, vintage shops, and live music.
- **Must-Visit Spot**: **The Hammered Lamb** (1235 N Orange Ave; Coordinates: 28.5596, -81.3722), known for its creative cocktails and friendly vibe.

Orlando's Best Restaurants

Orlando offers a wide variety of dining options beyond the tourist hotspots, and these restaurants showcase the diversity of flavors and cultural influences that make this city a culinary destination in its own right. From Cuban sandwiches and Southern comfort food to giant pizzas and Asian street food, Orlando's restaurant scene is sure to satisfy every palate, all while offering a relaxed, authentic dining experience. Whether you're a local or just visiting, these spots provide a taste of Orlando that's truly unforgettable.

1. The Ravenous Pig

- **Cuisine**: Modern American with a Southern twist
- **Average Price**: $15–$30 per entrée
- **Why Visit**: This beloved gastropub in Winter Park serves seasonal dishes with locally sourced ingredients. The menu changes regularly based on what's available, but favorites like their duck confit and house-made charcuterie remain staples. The creative cocktails and in-house brewed beers further enhance the experience.
- **Contact**: 565 W Fairbanks Ave, Winter Park, Florida 32789 | +1 407-628-2333
- **Website**: theravenouspig.com

2. Hawkers Asian Street Fare

- **Cuisine**: Asian fusion (street food-inspired)
- **Average Price**: $10–$20 per dish
- **Why Visit**: Located in the Mills 50 District, this restaurant brings the flavors of Southeast Asia to Orlando with a modern twist. The ambiance is casual, and the menu is packed with shareable dishes like bao buns, dumplings, and noodle bowls. The bar also serves creative cocktails with an Asian flair.

- **Contact**: 1103 N Mills Ave, Orlando, Florida 32803 | +1 407-704-8018
- **Website**: hawkersorlando.com

3. The Colonial Room Restaurant

- **Cuisine**: American (Southern comfort food)
- **Average Price**: $10–$20 per entrée
- **Why Visit**: Located inside the historic **Polk County Courthouse**, this charming spot offers a hearty taste of Southern classics, like chicken and waffles, shrimp and grits, and meatloaf. It's a throwback to the past with vintage décor and a warm, welcoming atmosphere, making it a popular spot for locals and visitors alike.
- **Contact**: 111 W Dakin Ave, Kissimmee, Florida 34741 | +1 407-847-6677
- **Website**: colonialroom.com

4. 4 Rivers Smokehouse

- **Cuisine**: Barbecue (Southern)
- **Average Price**: $8–$18 per plate
- **Why Visit**: A local institution, 4 Rivers is famous for its tender, smoked meats, particularly the brisket and pulled pork. The rustic décor and laid-back vibe make it the perfect place to indulge in comfort food. They also offer a variety of delicious sides like macaroni and cheese and fried okra.
- **Contact**: 1600 W Fairbanks Ave, Winter Park, Florida 32789 | +1 407-474-8377
- **Website**: 4riverssmokehouse.com

5. Black Bean Deli

- **Cuisine**: Cuban

- **Average Price**: $8–$15 per entrée
- **Why Visit**: For a taste of Cuban cuisine, head to **Black Bean Deli** in the College Park area. This spot is known for its sandwiches (especially the Cuban sandwich), ropa vieja, and, of course, its black beans and rice. The atmosphere is casual, with bright colors and a welcoming vibe, making it a great place for a quick, flavorful meal.
- **Contact**: 1231 N Orange Ave, Orlando, Florida 32804 | +1 407-872-5200
- **Website**: blackbeandeli.com

6. Se7en Bites

- **Cuisine**: Southern comfort (brunch-focused)
- **Average Price**: $10–$18 per dish
- **Why Visit**: A favorite for brunch lovers, Se7en Bites offers Southern-inspired comfort food with a modern twist. Signature dishes like their fried chicken and biscuit sandwiches, as well as the decadent s'mores pancakes, make this a must-visit for breakfast or brunch. The cozy ambiance and welcoming service enhance its overall appeal.
- **Contact**: 617 N Primrose Dr, Orlando, Florida 32803 | +1 407-203-0727
- **Website**: se7enbites.com

7. Tasty Chomps

- **Cuisine**: International street food
- **Average Price**: $5–$15 per item
- **Why Visit**: Tasty Chomps offers a rotating selection of street food-inspired offerings from around the world, served at food trucks or pop-ups around the Orlando area. From Mexican tacos to Filipino lumpia and everything in between, this is the place for adventurous eaters who want to try something new in a casual setting.

- **Contact**: Locations vary; follow on social media for the latest updates.
- **Website**: tastychomps.com

8. Lazy Moon Pizza

- **Cuisine**: Pizza (Italian)
- **Average Price**: $8–$16 per pizza
- **Why Visit**: Lazy Moon Pizza is famous for its giant slices of pizza, which are perfect for sharing or indulging solo. The atmosphere is relaxed and fun, with local art on the walls and a lively crowd. The extensive toppings list and crispy thin crust make it a must-try for pizza lovers in Orlando.
- **Contact**: 11551 University Blvd, Orlando, Florida 32817 | +1 407-275-0505
- **Website**: lazymoonpizza.com

9. Athenian Room

- **Cuisine**: Greek
- **Average Price**: $10–$20 per dish
- **Why Visit**: The Athenian Room is a beloved spot for fresh, flavorful Greek cuisine in a cozy setting. Their gyro plates, lamb chops, and tzatziki sauce are favorites among locals. With its laid-back vibe and long history in Orlando, it's a great place to enjoy a casual meal with excellent service.
- **Contact**: 1400 N Mills Ave, Orlando, Florida 32803 | +1 407-898-1010
- **Website**: athenianroom.com

10. The Smiling Bison

- **Cuisine**: American (farm-to-table)
- **Average Price**: $12–$22 per entrée

- **Why Visit**: The Smiling Bison focuses on serving locally sourced, farm-to-table dishes in a casual but creative atmosphere. Their seasonal menu changes regularly, with a focus on sustainability and inventive flavor combinations. Their bison burger is a must-try!
- **Contact**: 745 Bennett Rd, Orlando, Florida 32803 | +1 407-896-7246
- **Website**: thesmilingbison.com

Orlando's Best Hotels

Orlando is home to a variety of hotels that cater to different types of travelers, offering unique amenities, convenient locations, and affordable rates. Whether you're visiting for the theme parks, a business trip, or just to enjoy the vibrant city, here are some of the best hotels that provide a great balance of comfort, style, and value:

1. The Drury Inn & Suites Orlando

- **Location**: 7301 W Sand Lake Rd, Orlando, Florida 32819
- **Description**: This affordable and family-friendly hotel offers complimentary breakfast and evening snacks. It's located near famous theme parks, including Universal Studios, and provides an outdoor pool, fitness center, and free Wi-Fi. With spacious rooms and a warm atmosphere, it's perfect for a relaxed stay without breaking the bank.
- **Why Stay**: Guests can enjoy free hot breakfast, evening drinks and snacks, and convenient access to Universal Studios and other attractions.
- **Contact**: +1 407-354-1101
- **Website**: druryhotels.com

2. The Alfond Inn

- **Location**: 300 E New England Ave, Winter Park, Florida 32789
- **Description**: Located in the charming Winter Park district, The Alfond Inn offers a boutique experience with artistic flair. This mid-range hotel is surrounded by museums, parks, and charming local shops. It also features an on-site restaurant, a beautiful pool area, and art installations throughout the hotel, making it perfect for those looking to enjoy a cultural experience.

- **Why Stay**: Perfect for art lovers, the hotel has a stunning art collection and provides an ideal base for exploring Winter Park's local attractions.
- **Contact**: +1 407-645-6688
- **Website**: thealfondinn.com

3. Waldorf Astoria Orlando

- **Location**: 14200 Bonnet Creek Resort Ln, Orlando, Florida 32821
- **Description**: A luxurious option located in the Bonnet Creek area, this hotel offers high-end amenities like a golf course, spa services, and fine dining restaurants. While it's on the more expensive side, it's perfect for those seeking a luxurious experience, with beautifully decorated rooms and a tranquil atmosphere.
- **Why Stay**: If you're looking for a luxury experience that's not too far from the theme parks, Waldorf Astoria offers an ideal combination of convenience and indulgence.
- **Contact**: +1 407-597-5500
- **Website**: waldorfastoriaorlando.com

4. The Crowne Plaza Orlando

- **Location**: 7800 Universal Blvd, Orlando, Florida 32819
- **Description**: Located near Universal Studios, the Crowne Plaza Orlando provides guests with comfortable rooms and family-friendly amenities. The hotel features a range of amenities, including an outdoor pool, fitness center, and multiple on-site dining options. Its prime location makes it a perfect choice for those planning to visit nearby theme parks or explore downtown Orlando.
- **Why Stay**: Its central location and family-friendly environment make it an ideal option for those who want to visit the theme parks while enjoying comfortable accommodations.

- **Contact**: +1 407-996-9840
- **Website**: ihg.com

5. Disney's Art of Animation Resort

- **Location**: 1850 Animation Way, Lake Buena Vista, Florida 32830
- **Description**: A Disney hotel that's ideal for families, this resort immerses guests in the world of animation with larger-than-life designs based on Disney movies like *The Lion King* and *Finding Nemo*. It offers spacious rooms, family suites, and a fun atmosphere for kids of all ages. With an outdoor pool and a food court offering casual dining options, it's perfect for families looking to stay within a Disney experience.
- **Why Stay**: This resort is highly themed, making it a fantastic choice for Disney fans and families with young children who want a magical, immersive experience.
- **Contact**: +1 407-938-7000
- **Website**: disneyworld.disney.go.com

6. The Four Seasons Resort Orlando

- **Location**: 10100 Dream Tree Blvd, Orlando, Florida 32836
- **Description**: Situated within the Golden Oak neighborhood near Walt Disney World, the Four Seasons offers luxury accommodations that cater to families, couples, and those seeking a high-end getaway. With an on-site water park, spa, golf course, and exceptional dining options, it's an idyllic retreat for those looking to splurge.
- **Why Stay**: For those who want an upscale stay with the best in service, amenities, and a family-friendly environment, the Four Seasons offers an unforgettable Orlando experience.
- **Contact**: +1 407-313-7777
- **Website**: fourseasons.com

7. Universal's Cabana Bay Beach Resort

- **Location**: 6550 Adventure Way, Orlando, Florida 32819
- **Description**: A retro-style resort located right next to Universal Studios, this hotel offers a fun, relaxed atmosphere with a nostalgic 1950s and 1960s vibe. The Cabana Bay Beach Resort has affordable rates for families while offering fantastic amenities such as a lazy river pool, bowling alley, and a food court. It's an affordable option for guests visiting the Universal parks.
- **Why Stay**: The nostalgic design and family-friendly atmosphere make this an ideal base for guests wanting to experience Universal Studios and nearby attractions.
- **Contact**: +1 407-503-4000
- **Website**: universalorlando.com

8. The Kissimmee Bay Hotel

- **Location**: 1805 Hotel Plaza Blvd, Kissimmee, Florida 34747
- **Description**: A more affordable hotel just a short drive from Disney World, The Kissimmee Bay Hotel offers an outdoor pool, casual dining options, and cozy rooms. It's ideal for travelers who want a comfortable stay near the parks without paying the high prices of on-property hotels.
- **Why Stay**: For families on a budget, this hotel offers great proximity to the parks and a relaxed atmosphere.
- **Contact**: +1 407-239-1444
- **Website**: kissimmeebayhotel.com

9. The Wyndham Grand Orlando Resort Bonnet Creek

- **Location**: 14651 Chelonia Pkwy, Orlando, Florida 32821
- **Description**: Situated in a scenic, peaceful area near Disney Springs, this resort features beautiful lakeside views and high-end amenities such as an outdoor pool, full-

service spa, and several dining options. The resort's rooms are spacious, and it provide a tranquil experience away from the hustle and bustle of the theme parks.
- **Why Stay**: Ideal for travelers seeking a relaxed, scenic stay with proximity to Walt Disney World.
- **Contact**: +1 407-390-2300

Lesser-known Gems in Central Florida

While Orlando, with its world-famous theme parks, draws the bulk of Central Florida's tourism, there are quieter, less commercialized destinations in the region that are equally captivating. Two such hidden gems are **Bok Tower Gardens** and the **freshwater springs of Ocala**, each offering unique opportunities for relaxation, exploration, and nature immersion.

Bok Tower Gardens: A Hidden Oasis of Beauty and Tranquility

Located in **Lake Wales**, Bok Tower Gardens is one of Central Florida's most serene and beautiful spots, known for its stunning botanical gardens and the grand **Pinewood Estate**. This national historic landmark, established in 1929 by **Edward W. Bok**, is a testament to his vision of creating a peaceful place that promotes reflection and connection with nature. The iconic **Bok Tower** itself is an architectural masterpiece that soars 205 feet into the sky, surrounded by lush gardens, flowering plants, and peaceful walking paths.

Why Visit: Bok Tower Gardens offers a peaceful retreat from the hustle and bustle, providing visitors with an opportunity to stroll through beautifully designed gardens and enjoy spectacular views. The **Singing Tower** carillon chimes throughout the day, adding a musical touch to the experience. The gardens themselves feature a variety of landscapes, from tropical and subtropical to wildflower meadows and serene water features.

Noteworthy Features:

Singing Tower Carillon: The tower features one of the world's finest carillons, with 60 bells that ring out several times a day, offering a unique musical experience.

- **Pinewood Estate**: A 20-room mansion built in the 1930s that showcases Mediterranean Revival-style architecture, complete with gardens and scenic views.
- **Bird Watching and Nature Trails**: The grounds are home to a variety of birds, and the walking trails allow for peaceful exploration of the natural surroundings.

Contact Information:

- **Address**: 1151 Tower Blvd, Lake Wales, Florida 33853
- **Phone**: +1 863-676-1408
- **Website**: Bok Tower Gardens

The Freshwater Springs of Ocala: A Natural Wonderland

Ocala, located in the heart of Florida, is home to an impressive collection of **freshwater springs**, many of which are part of the **Ocala National Forest**. These springs are not only essential to the region's ecosystem but also provide excellent opportunities for outdoor activities, from kayaking and canoeing to wildlife watching and simply enjoying the pristine beauty of nature.

Why Visit: The springs of Ocala are lesser-known compared to the more famous springs in Florida, but they offer an equally stunning experience. These clear, spring-fed waters create picturesque swimming holes and sparkling rivers, ideal for a day of exploration and relaxation. The springs provide a refreshing escape, and the surrounding forest provides a natural backdrop for hiking, picnicking, and photography.

Notable Springs to Explore:

1. **Silver Springs State Park**:
   - One of the most iconic springs in the state, Silver Springs has a long history as a popular tourist attraction, offering glass-bottom boat tours of the spring's crystal-clear waters.

- o **Why It's Special**: Silver Springs is famous for its clarity, making it a great place to observe aquatic life, and the surrounding park provides opportunities for hiking and wildlife observation.
- o **Coordinates**: 29.2081° N, 82.0226° W
- o **Address**: 1425 NE 58th Ave, Ocala, Florida 34470
- o **Phone**: +1 352-236-7148
- o **Website**: Silver Springs State Park

2. **Juniper Springs**:
   - o Located deep within the Ocala National Forest, **Juniper Springs** is one of the oldest and most popular spring sites in Florida. Visitors can enjoy canoeing or kayaking along Juniper Creek or simply relax in the cool waters of the spring itself.
   - o **Why It's Special**: The spring is surrounded by lush, forested landscapes and is home to a historic mill that dates back to the 1930s.
   - o **Coordinates**: 29.0085° N, 81.6550° W
   - o **Address**: 26701 FL-40, Silver Springs, Florida 34488
   - o **Phone**: +1 352-625-2808
   - o **Website**: Juniper Springs Recreation Area

3. **Alexander Springs**:
   - o Alexander Springs is a beautiful spring within the Ocala National Forest, offering a tranquil environment for swimming, snorkeling, and paddling. The spring's water flows into a picturesque pool, surrounded by tall cypress trees and lush vegetation.
   - o **Why It's Special**: The spring provides a peaceful, uncrowded experience compared to other springs, with some of the clearest water in Florida.
   - o **Coordinates**: 29.0862° N, 81.5967° W
   - o **Address**: 49525 County Rd 445, Altoona, Florida 32702
   - o **Phone**: +1 352-669-3522
   - o **Website**: Alexander Springs Recreation Area

Orlando in Three Days

Orlando offers much more than just its renowned theme parks. The city and its surrounding areas are brimming with diverse experiences, from cultural attractions and outdoor adventures to opportunities for relaxation, making it a perfect destination for visitors seeking a well-rounded vacation. Here's an exciting three-day itinerary that gives you the best of both worlds: the famous Orlando attractions mixed with lesser-known gems.

Day 1: Iconic Orlando Attractions & Relaxing Evening

Morning:

- **Start with a Visit to the Magic Kingdom:** Begin your Orlando adventure at the most iconic of Disney theme parks, the **Magic Kingdom**. It's where fairy tales come to life, with its famous Cinderella Castle at the heart of the park. While most visitors flock here for rides like Space Mountain and Pirates of the Caribbean, there are also opportunities to enjoy some classic Disney experiences, such as character meet-and-greets or parades.
    - **Coordinates**: 28.4187° N, 81.5812° W
    - **Tip**: Arrive early to catch the popular rides with shorter wait times.

Lunch:

- **Columbia Restaurant** (Celebration)After a morning at Magic Kingdom, take a short drive to the charming town of **Celebration** (about 20 minutes) and enjoy lunch at the **Columbia Restaurant**, an Orlando staple for Cuban cuisine.
    - **Address**: 649 Front St, Celebration, Florida 34747
    - **Cuisine**: Cuban, Spanish
    - **Average Price**: $$-$$$

- **Phone**: +1 407-938-9001

Afternoon:

- **Explore Disney Springs** After lunch, head to **Disney Springs**, a vibrant entertainment district. Take a stroll around the waterfront, visit unique shops, and perhaps catch a show at **House of Blues**. It's the perfect way to enjoy Orlando's shopping, dining, and entertainment without the theme park crowds.
    - **Coordinates**: 28.3702° N, 81.5158° W

Evening:

- **Relax at Lake Eola Park** To wrap up your first day, unwind at **Lake Eola Park**, located in downtown Orlando. This peaceful spot is perfect for a relaxing stroll or a boat ride on the lake. You can rent a swan-shaped paddle boat or simply enjoy the serene views of the downtown skyline. It's a lovely place to watch the sunset and enjoy the beauty of nature.
    - **Coordinates**: 28.5410° N, 81.3792° W

Dinner:

- **The Boathouse** (Disney Springs) For dinner, head back to **Disney Springs** and dine at **The Boathouse**, a waterfront restaurant known for its fresh seafood and American classics. The laid-back yet vibrant atmosphere makes it perfect for a relaxing evening meal. You can even enjoy a drink at the outdoor bar, which overlooks the lake.
    - **Address**: 1620 E Buena Vista Dr, Lake Buena Vista, Florida 32830
    - **Cuisine**: Seafood, American
    - **Average Price**: $$-$$$
    - **Phone**: +1 407-939-2628

Day 2: Nature and Culture in Orlando

Morning:

- **Visit Leu Gardens** Begin your second day in Orlando with a visit to **Harry P. Leu Gardens**, a stunning 50-acre garden located just a few minutes from downtown. The gardens are a peaceful escape with beautiful landscapes, including azaleas, roses, and a butterfly garden. This is a great spot for a relaxing morning stroll.
    - **Coordinates**: 28.6039° N, 81.3659° W
    - **Admission**: Adults $10, Children $5
    - **Phone**: +1 407-246-2620

Lunch:

- **East End Market** After exploring the gardens, head over to **East End Market**, a trendy food market that features local vendors selling everything from fresh produce to gourmet sandwiches and baked goods. You'll find a variety of casual dining options here to enjoy while soaking in the hip atmosphere.
    - **Address**: 3201 Corrine Dr, Orlando, Florida 32803
    - **Cuisine**: American, Local, Variety
    - **Average Price**: $
    - **Phone**: +1 407-757-0992

Afternoon:

- **Orlando Museum of Art** For a taste of Orlando's artistic side, spend your afternoon at the **Orlando Museum of Art**, located near Loch Haven Park. The museum showcases contemporary art exhibits as well as regional and international artists. Don't miss their permanent collection of American art, which is rich in history and culture.
    - **Coordinates**: 28.5594° N, 81.3756° W
    - **Admission**: Adults $15, Children $5
    - **Phone**: +1 407-896-4231

Evening:

- **Dinner at The Ravenous Pig** For dinner, enjoy a hearty meal at **The Ravenous Pig**, a gastropub in Winter Park, just outside downtown Orlando. Known for its upscale pub food and seasonal menu, this spot offers dishes like duck confit, pork belly, and homemade sausages.
    - **Address**: 565 W Fairbanks Ave, Winter Park, Florida 32789
    - **Cuisine**: Gastropub, American
    - **Average Price**: $$-$$$
    - **Phone**: +1 407-628-2333

Night Activity:

- **Dr. Phillips Center for the Performing Arts** If you're in the mood for a night of culture, check out a performance at the **Dr. Phillips Center for the Performing Arts**. Whether it's a Broadway show, ballet, or concert, this venue offers a variety of performances throughout the year.
    - **Coordinates**: 28.5409° N, 81.3812° W
    - **Phone**: +1 407-839-0119

Day 3: Exploring the Surroundings of Orlando

Morning:

- **Bok Tower Gardens** (Lake Wales) Begin your final day with a visit to **Bok Tower Gardens**, located about an hour south of Orlando. This serene garden offers beautifully landscaped grounds, peaceful walking paths, and the iconic 205-foot singing tower. The gardens are a great place to relax and enjoy nature's beauty.
    - **Coordinates**: 27.9271° N, 81.5836° W
    - **Admission**: Adults $15, Children $5
    - **Phone**: +1 863-676-1408

Lunch:

- **The Barn at Bok Tower Gardens** Enjoy a rustic lunch at **The Barn** located on the grounds of Bok Tower Gardens. They offer casual fare like sandwiches, soups, and salads in a charming, relaxed environment. It's an ideal spot to relax and rejuvenate after touring the gardens.
    - **Address**: 1151 Tower Blvd, Lake Wales, Florida 33853
    - **Cuisine**: American, Casual
    - **Average Price**: $$
    - **Phone**: +1 863-676-1408

Afternoon:

- **Blue Spring State Park**

After lunch, head to **Blue Spring State Park** near Orange City. This beautiful state park is known for its crystal-clear spring and manatee viewing opportunities in the winter months. Visitors can also enjoy hiking trails, canoeing, and picnicking along the St. Johns River.

    - **Coordinates**: 28.9911° N, 81.3489° W
    - **Admission**: $6 per vehicle
    - **Phone**: +1 386-775-3663

Evening:

- **Dinner at El Patron** Finish your day with a flavorful meal at **El Patron** in Winter Park. This lively Mexican restaurant is perfect for a relaxed dinner with flavorful tacos, enchiladas, and fajitas. Enjoy their margaritas and fresh salsas while soaking up the festive ambiance.
    - **Address**: 153 E New England Ave, Winter Park, Florida 32789
    - **Cuisine**: Mexican
    - **Average Price**: $$-$$$
    - **Phone**: +1 407-796-7277

THE SPACE COAST

A Gateway to the Stars and More

The Space Coast, aptly named for its close ties to America's space exploration history, is a stretch of Florida's eastern coastline that offers a fascinating blend of history, natural beauty, and unique attractions. This region, spanning about 72 miles along the Atlantic Ocean, is primarily anchored by Brevard County and features iconic sites like Cape Canaveral and Kennedy Space Center, along with stunning beaches, charming towns, and pristine wildlife preserves.

Historical Trivia

The Space Coast is synonymous with space exploration. It gained prominence in the late 1950s and 1960s as NASA established its operations at Cape Canaveral, a site chosen for its proximity to the equator, which allows rockets to take advantage of Earth's rotational speed. The first human spaceflight mission, Apollo 7, launched from here in 1968, followed by the legendary Apollo 11 moon landing mission in 1969. Visitors can immerse themselves in this rich history by visiting the **Kennedy Space Center Visitor Complex**, where they can explore exhibits, touch moon rocks, and even meet astronauts.

Less commonly known is that before its space era, this area thrived on industries like citrus farming and fishing. Cape Canaveral was once called Cape Canaveral Lighthouse Reservation in the 1800s, guiding ships navigating these Atlantic waters.

Land Features and Climate

The Space Coast boasts a dynamic landscape that includes sandy beaches, barrier islands, lagoons, and estuaries teeming with wildlife. The centerpiece of the region is the Indian River Lagoon, renowned as one of the most ecologically diverse estuaries in North

America, supporting over 4,300 species of flora and fauna. Its subtropical climate offers warm, humid summers and pleasant, mild winters, making it an inviting destination no matter the season.

The region experiences a subtropical climate, characterized by hot, humid summers and mild winters, making it an ideal destination to visit throughout the year. Summer months are great for beachgoers and surfers, while cooler winter temperatures (rarely below 50°F) attract those who enjoy hiking and birdwatching.

Key Places to Visit

1. **Kennedy Space Center Visitor Complex**
    o The most iconic attraction on the Space Coast, it offers interactive exhibits, shuttle launch simulations, and the Space Shuttle Atlantis on display. Don't miss the Rocket Garden or the bus tour to the Apollo/Saturn V Center.
2. **Cocoa Beach**
    o Known for its laid-back vibe, Cocoa Beach is a surfer's paradise and home to the famous Ron Jon Surf Shop. Relax on the beach, visit the Cocoa Beach Pier for fresh seafood, or catch a rocket launch view right from the sand.
    o **Coordinates**: 28.3200° N, 80.6076° W
3. **Canaveral National Seashore**
    o A lesser-known treasure, this pristine stretch of coastline features undeveloped beaches, dunes, and lagoons. It's an ideal retreat for those who cherish nature and crave tranquility. Hike along scenic trails or spot nesting sea turtles during summer.
    o **Coordinates**: 28.7886° N, 80.7496° W
4. **Merritt Island National Wildlife Refuge**
    o Located near the Kennedy Space Center, this refuge is perfect for birdwatching, kayaking, and observing alligators in their natural habitat. The

Black Point Wildlife Drive offers a scenic way to explore the wetlands.
- **Coordinates**: 28.6360° N, 80.7500° W
5. **Historic Cocoa Village**
    - A charming, walkable area filled with unique shops, art galleries, and cafes. It's also home to the historic Cocoa Village Playhouse, which has been entertaining locals since 1924.
    - **Coordinates**: 28.3550° N, 80.7250° W
6. **Sebastian Inlet State Park**
    - This hidden gem is a haven for anglers, surfers, and beachcombers. The park is home to two fascinating museums the Sebastian Fishing Museum, and : the McLarty Treasure Museum
    - **Coordinates**: 27.8573° N, 80.4473° W
7. **Port Canaveral**
    - Not just a cruise hub, this port area offers waterfront dining, deep-sea fishing excursions, and the Exploration Tower, where you can enjoy panoramic views of the coast.
8. **Satellite Beach**
    - A quieter alternative to Cocoa Beach, Satellite Beach is ideal for families. Its clean, serene beaches and local parks make it perfect for picnics and relaxing by the ocean.
    - **Coordinates**: 28.1760° N, 80.5903° W

Lesser-Known Gems

- **Playalinda Beach** (Part of Canaveral National Seashore): A tranquil, undeveloped beach perfect for those seeking peace and quiet. It's also a prime spot to watch rocket launches.
    - **Coordinates**: 28.6650° N, 80.6380° W
- **Enchanted Forest Sanctuary**: Located in Titusville, this small nature preserve offers peaceful hiking trails that meander through oak hammocks and wetlands.
    - **Coordinates**: 28.5720° N, 80.8266° W

One-Day Itinerary in Cape Canaveral

A Perfect Blend of Space, Nature, and Coastal Charm

Cape Canaveral offers a unique combination of space exploration history, natural beauty, and coastal charm, making it a must-visit destination on Florida's Space Coast. Here's a carefully curated one-day itinerary designed for an enjoyable and seamless experience.

Morning: Dive into Space Exploration

Stop 1: Kennedy Space Center Visitor Complex

Kickstart your day at the iconic Kennedy Space Center Visitor Complex. Explore exhibits that celebrate the past, present, and future of space exploration. Highlights include the Rocket Garden, the Space Shuttle Atlantis exhibit, and the Heroes and Legends Hall of Fame. You can also take the guided bus tour to the Apollo/Saturn V Center, where the massive Saturn V rocket is displayed.

- **Location**: Space Commerce Way, Merritt Island, Florida 32953
- **Hours**: 9:00 AM - 5:00 PM
- **Admission**: Starts at $75 for adults
- **Website**: Kennedy Space Center Visitor Complex
- **Contact**: (855) 433-4210

Lunch: Dining Near the Stars

Stop 2: Orbit Café

Conveniently located within the Kennedy Space Center, this casual dining option offers a variety of American-style dishes, including burgers, salads, and vegetarian options. The space-themed décor adds to the experience, making it a fun place for a quick lunch before continuing your exploration.

- **Location**: Inside Kennedy Space Center
- **Average Price**: $10-$15 per meal
- **Contact**: (855) 433-4210

Early Afternoon: Coastal Adventures

Stop 3: Exploration Tower

After lunch, head to Exploration Tower at Port Canaveral, a short drive from the Kennedy Space Center. This architectural gem offers panoramic views of the Space Coast from its observation deck. Inside, you'll find interactive exhibits on the area's maritime history, shipping operations, and space exploration.

- **Location**: 670 Dave Nisbet Dr, Cape Canaveral, Florida 32920
- **Hours**: 10:00 AM - 5:00 PM
- **Admission**: $6.50 for adults
- **Contact**: (321) 394-3408

Late Afternoon: Relax on the Beach

Stop 4: Cherie Down Park

Spend your late afternoon soaking up the sun at Cherie Down Park, a quieter, lesser-known beach. This family-friendly spot features clean sand, calm waters, and picnic pavilions. It's perfect for a leisurely walk or simply relaxing by the ocean.

- **Location**: 8330 Ridgewood Ave, Cape Canaveral, Florida 32920
- **Hours**: Sunrise to Sunset
- **Contact**: (321) 455-1380

Dinner: Coastal Dining

Stop 5: Grills Seafood Deck & Tiki Bar

Cap off your day with a waterfront dinner at Grills Seafood Deck & Tiki Bar. This laid-back restaurant offers fresh seafood, steak, and tropical drinks, all served with views of Port Canaveral's bustling waterways. You might even catch a cruise ship departing!

- **Location**: 505 Glen Cheek Dr, Cape Canaveral, Florida 32920
- **Average Price**: $15-$25 per meal
- **Contact**: (321) 868-2226

Evening: Sunset and Stargazing

Stop 6: Jetty Park

End your day at Jetty Park, a scenic spot for watching the sunset over the Atlantic Ocean. The pier offers fantastic views and is a popular location for spotting dolphins and manatees. After sunset, stay a while for some stargazing—the dark skies of Cape Canaveral are perfect for it.

- **Location**: 400 Jetty Park Rd, Cape Canaveral, Florida 32920
- **Hours**: 7:00 AM - 9:00 PM
- **Admission**: $5 per vehicle
- **Contact**: (321) 783-7111

Pro Tips

- Wear comfortable walking shoes as you'll be on your feet most of the day.
- Bring sunscreen and a hat for the beach and outdoor activities.
- Check rocket launch schedules ahead of time for a chance to witness a live launch from Cape Canaveral during your visit.

Three-Day Itinerary: Hidden Gems of The Space Coast

This three-day itinerary focuses on lesser-visited gems, from nature reserves and pristine beaches to charming towns and unique outdoor experiences.

Day 1: Natural Wonders and Wildlife

Morning: Black Point Wildlife Drive (Merritt Island National Wildlife Refuge)

Kick off your adventure with a scenic drive through the Merritt Island National Wildlife Refuge. The 7-mile Black Point Wildlife Drive offers opportunities to see native wildlife such as alligators, manatees, and over 300 species of birds. Bring binoculars for birdwatching and enjoy several short trails along the route.

- **Location**: 1987 Scrub Jay Way, Titusville, Florida 32782
- **Hours**: Sunrise to sunset
- **Admission**: $10 per vehicle
- **Contact**: (321) 861-0667

Lunch: Dixie Crossroads

Savor fresh seafood at this local favorite in Titusville. Their famous rock shrimp and fried green tomatoes are a must-try, and they offer an array of casual dining options in a cozy setting.

- **Location**: 1475 Garden St, Titusville, Florida 32796
- **Average Price**: $15-$25 per meal
- **Contact**: (321) 268-5000

Afternoon: Enchanted Forest Sanctuary

Explore this peaceful, lesser-known nature preserve that features a variety of habitats, from oak scrub to wetlands. Walk the shaded trails and enjoy the serene beauty of Florida's native plants and wildlife.

- **Location**: 444 Columbia Blvd, Titusville, Florida 32780
- **Hours**: 9:00 AM - 5:00 PM
- **Admission**: Free
- **Contact**: (321) 264-5185

Evening: Sunset at Parrish Park

End the day with a stunning sunset at Parrish Park, located on the banks of the Indian River. This quiet spot is perfect for relaxing by the water while watching the sky light up in hues of orange and pink.

- **Location**: 1 A. Max Brewer Memorial Pkwy, Titusville, Florida 32796
- **Admission**: Free

Day 2: Pristine Beaches and Coastal Charm

Morning: Playalinda Beach (Canaveral National Seashore)

Escape to this unspoiled beach, known for its natural beauty and tranquility. Ideal for a morning walk or a swim, it's a favorite among locals who want to avoid crowded tourist spots.

- **Location**: Playalinda Beach Rd, Titusville, Florida 32796
- **Hours**: 6:00 AM - 8:00 PM
- **Admission**: $20 per vehicle (valid for 7 days)
- **Contact**: (321) 267-1110

Lunch: Third Culture Kitchen

Enjoy a fusion of global flavors at this casual eatery in Titusville. From bao buns to poke bowls, their creative dishes and friendly atmosphere make it a standout spot.

- **Location**: 1000 Cheney Hwy, Titusville, Florida 32780
- **Average Price**: $10-$20 per meal
- **Contact**: (321) 567-6041

Afternoon: Melbourne Beach Pier

Head south to Melbourne Beach, where you can explore the historic Melbourne Beach Pier. Built in 1889, this wooden pier extends into the Indian River Lagoon and offers beautiful views, fishing opportunities, and a slice of history.

- **Location**: Ocean Ave, Melbourne Beach, Florida 32951
- **Admission**: Free

Dinner: Ocean 302

Located near Melbourne Beach, this relaxed gastropub serves delicious, locally sourced meals. Their wood-fired pizzas pair perfectly with their selection of craft beers, making them a must-try.

- **Location**: 302 Ocean Ave, Melbourne Beach, Florida 32951
- **Average Price**: $15-$30 per meal
- **Contact**: (321) 802-5728

Day 3: Small-Town Charm and Adventure

Morning: Historic Cocoa Village

Begin your day in the charming Cocoa Village, known for its quaint streets lined with boutique shops, art galleries, and historic buildings. Visit the Cocoa Village Playhouse, which has been entertaining visitors since 1924, and enjoy a morning coffee at a local café.

- **Location**: Brevard Ave, Cocoa, Florida 32922
- **Hours**: Shops typically open 10:00 AM - 5:00 PM

Lunch: Ryan's Village Pizza & Pub

Grab a casual lunch at this beloved pizza joint in Cocoa Village. Known for its hearty pies and relaxed atmosphere, it's perfect for refueling before your afternoon activities.

- **Location**: 405 Delannoy Ave, Cocoa, Florida32922
- **Average Price**: $10-$15 per meal
- **Contact**: (321) 633-1211

Afternoon: Lone Cabbage Fish Camp (Airboat Adventure)

Experience an authentic Florida airboat ride at Lone Cabbage Fish Camp. Glide through the St. Johns River marshlands, spot alligators, and immerse yourself in the wild beauty of the area.

- **Location**: 8199 W King St, Cocoa, Florida32926
- **Hours**: 10:00 AM - 6:00 PM
- **Airboat Rides**: $30-$50 per person
- **Contact**: (321) 632-4199

Dinner: Grills Seafood Deck & Tiki Bar (Cocoa)

End your Space Coast adventure with a relaxed waterfront dinner at Grills Seafood Deck in Cocoa. Enjoy fresh seafood, live music, and a picturesque view of the Banana River.

- **Location**: 505 Glen Cheek Dr, Cape Canaveral, Florida32920
- **Average Price**: $15-$30 per meal
- **Contact**: (321) 868-2226

SOUTH FLORIDA

South Florida, a vibrant tapestry of history, culture, and natural beauty, offers visitors an array of experiences that blend its rich past with contemporary allure.

Historical and Artistic Relics

South Florida's history is deeply rooted in its diverse cultural influences, from Native American heritage to Spanish colonialism and beyond. This rich past is reflected in numerous historical sites and artistic landmarks that offer a glimpse into the region's storied background.

- **Vizcaya Museum and Gardens**: Located in Miami, this early 20th-century estate showcases European-inspired architecture and lush gardens, providing insight into the opulent lifestyle of its era.
- **Deering Estate**: Also in Miami, the Deering Estate is a historic landmark that offers guided tours through its historic houses and nature preserves, showcasing archaeological treasures and eco-marvels.
- **Old Fort Lauderdale Village and Museum**: This charming collection of historic buildings includes the King-Cromartie House (circa 1907) and New River Inn (circa 1905), offering a glimpse into the early days of Fort Lauderdale and Broward County.
- **Jupiter Inlet Lighthouse & Museum**: A historic lighthouse offering tours and exhibits about the area's maritime history.
- **Key Biscayne**: Home to the historic Cape Florida Lighthouse, Key Biscayne offers a serene escape with its beautiful beaches and nature parks.

Climate and Best Time to Visit

South Florida boasts a tropical climate, offering warm weather throughout the year. From November to April, the region experiences a dry season, while the wet season lasts from May to October.

- **Peak Season (December to April):** This time is perfect for outdoor activities, with mild temperatures and low humidity, though it brings larger crowds and higher rates.
- **Shoulder Seasons (April-May, September-November):** Great for moderate weather, fewer tourists, and more budget-friendly accommodations.
- **Off-Season (June to August)**: Expect higher temperatures and increased humidity, along with a greater chance of afternoon thunderstorms. This period sees fewer tourists, which can be advantageous for those seeking a quieter visit.

Culinary Delights

The culinary scene in South Florida is a melting pot of flavors, influenced by Caribbean, Latin American, and Southern cuisines.

- **Seafood Delights:** With its prime coastal location, South Florida is a paradise for seafood lovers. Fresh catches like stone crabs, grouper, and mahi-mahi are celebrated in local dishes, often prepared with tropical flavors and unique seasonings that highlight the area's connection to the sea.
- **Cuban Cuisine**: Miami's Little Havana is renowned for authentic Cuban dishes, including the classic Cuban sandwich and ropa vieja.
- **Key Lime Pie**: A must-try dessert originating from the Florida Keys, offering a tangy and sweet treat.

Exploring Miami

A One-Day Itinerary for the Ultimate South Florida Experience

Miami is a city that thrives with vibrant energy, blending rich cultural diversity, stunning architecture, and natural beauty. Known for its glamorous beaches, iconic nightlife, and bustling art scene, Miami offers a little something for everyone. From the famous Art Deco District in South Beach to the lush greenery of its parks, Miami is an exciting mix of relaxation, exploration, and entertainment.

For those eager to experience the best of Miami in one day, this thoughtfully curated itinerary will guide you through the must-visit spots without wasting time in traffic or wandering too far from one place to the next. Prepare yourself for an exciting day filled with rich cultural experiences, fascinating history, mouthwatering cuisine, and breathtaking scenery.

Morning: Cultural Delights and Beautiful Views

Breakfast at Big Pink

Start your day with a hearty breakfast at Big Pink, a local favorite known for its extensive menu and classic American breakfast dishes. It's a great spot to fuel up before your adventures in the city. *Address:* 157 Collins Ave, Miami Beach, FL 33139 *Contact:* +1 305-532-4700

South Beach and Ocean Drive

After breakfast, head to South Beach. This iconic area is famous for its soft white sand and sparkling turquoise water. Walk along Ocean Drive to admire the colorful Art Deco buildings, or relax on the beach while soaking up the Miami sun. *Address for South Beach:* 1000 Ocean Dr, Miami Beach, FL 33139

Art Deco Historic District

From South Beach, take a short walk to explore the Art Deco Historic District. With over 800 preserved buildings, this area offers a fascinating glimpse into Miami's past. A guided walking tour is a great way to learn about the history and architecture of the district.
Address for Visitor Center: 1001 Ocean Dr, Miami Beach, FL 33139
Contact: +1 305-672-2014

Midday: Art, Nature, and Lunch with a View

Vizcaya Museum and Gardens

Next, head to the stunning Vizcaya Museum and Gardens, just a short drive from the beach. This historic mansion, built in the early 20th century, is surrounded by lush gardens that offer a peaceful escape from the city's hustle and bustle. The museum is filled with art and artifacts, making it a perfect stop for history and art lovers.
Address: 3251 S Miami Ave, Miami, FL 33129
Contact: +1 305-250-9133

Lunch at The Greenhouse Café

For lunch, head to The Greenhouse Cafe, a charming and affordable spot that serves fresh and healthy meals with an emphasis on locally sourced ingredients. The outdoor seating is perfect for a relaxing lunch break in a tranquil atmosphere.
Address: 1756 Collins Ave, Miami Beach, FL 33139
Contact: +1 305-672-2882

Afternoon: A Taste of Miami's Diversity

Little Havana and Calle Ocho

After lunch, make your way to Little Havana, the heart of Miami's Cuban community. Stroll along Calle Ocho, where you can find colorful murals, authentic Cuban restaurants, and lively street music. Make sure to visit Domino Park, where you can watch locals engage in lively games of dominoes and soak in the vibrant, energetic atmosphere. It's a great spot to experience the community spirit and enjoy the buzz of activity, making it a must-see for anyone wanting to truly feel the pulse of the area.

Address for Little Havana Visitor Center: 1400 SW 8th St, Miami, FL 33135

Contact: +1 305-643-5500

Wynwood Walls

Next, take a short drive to Wynwood Walls, a must-visit for art enthusiasts. This outdoor museum features massive murals painted by some of the world's most talented street artists. The colorful walls and unique art installations make this a perfect spot for photos and a taste of Miami's thriving art scene. *Address:* 2520 NW 2nd Ave, Miami, FL 33127 *Contact:* +1 305-531-4411

Evening: Sunset, Dinner, and Nightlife

Sunset at Bayfront Park

As the day begins to wind down, head to Bayfront Park for a serene sunset view over Biscayne Bay. The park offers beautiful walking paths, green spaces, and stunning views of the water and downtown Miami.

Address: 301 N Biscayne Blvd, Miami, FL 33132 *Contact:* +1 305-358-7550

Dinner at The Wharf Miami

For a casual yet delicious dinner, visit The Wharf Miami, a lively riverside venue offering a variety of food trucks and bars, plus a beautiful view of the Miami River. You can enjoy everything from tacos to fresh seafood while listening to live music. *Address:* 114 SW North River Dr, Miami, FL 33130 *Contact:* +1 305-906-4000

Nightlife at E11EVEN Miami

End your day with a night out in one of Miami's most famous nightclubs, E11EVEN. This 24/7 club is known for its exciting atmosphere, top DJs, and high-energy performances. It's the perfect way to experience Miami's nightlife in style. *Address:* 29 NE 11th St, Miami, FL 33132 *Contact:* +1 305-829-2911

Things to Remember:

- **Transportation:** Miami's public transportation system, including the MetroMover, is great for getting around, but taxis and ride-share services are also easily accessible. If you prefer to walk, many of these locations are within a short distance from each other.
- **Dress Code:** Miami is known for its casual yet fashionable vibe. Comfortable clothes and shoes are recommended for daytime activities, but don't forget to bring something stylish for dinner or the nightlife scene.

Must-Visit Cities in South Florida

Here are some of the most interesting cities to visit in South Florida, each offering unique experiences that cater to history lovers, nature enthusiasts, and culture seekers alike, after Miami:

1. Fort Lauderdale

Nicknamed the "Venice of America," Fort Lauderdale is a city of sparkling waterways, pristine beaches, and lively cultural districts. It's a destination where you can combine relaxation, adventure, and urban sophistication.

Key Attractions:

- **Las Olas Boulevard**: Serves as the bustling centerpiece of Fort Lauderdale's dining, shopping, and cultural scene. Take a leisurely stroll along this lively, picturesque street, where you'll discover an array of boutique shops, upscale restaurants offering a variety of cuisines, and captivating art galleries showcasing local and international talent. It's the perfect spot to experience the city's unique charm and vibrant energy.. Don't miss the charming sidewalk cafes perfect for people-watching.
- **Fort Lauderdale Beach**: A quieter, family-friendly alternative to Miami Beach. Its wide stretch of soft sand is perfect for sunbathing, while its calm waters invite swimmers and paddleboarders.
- **Bonnet House Museum & Gardens**: A hidden oasis of art and history surrounded by lush tropical gardens. Wander through the historic home and enjoy a peaceful escape from the city.
- **Water Taxi Tours**: Hop aboard a water taxi to explore the

- **Coordinates**: 26.1224° N, 80.1373° W
- **Hotels**:

- Tru by Hilton Fort Lauderdale Downtown
    - **Address**: 315 NW 1st Ave, Fort Lauderdale, FL 33301
    - **Contact**: +1 954-371-1700
    - A sleek, modern hotel offering free breakfast, a fitness center, and proximity to Las Olas Boulevard. Rooms start at ~$150/night.
- The Victoria Park Hotel
    - **Address**: 855 NE 20th Ave, Fort Lauderdale, FL 33304
    - **Contact**: +1 954-564-5952
    - A boutique hotel with a cozy atmosphere, outdoor pool, and tropical gardens. Rooms start at ~$120/night.

- **Restaurants**:
  - **Coconuts**
      - **Address**: 429 Seabreeze Blvd, Fort Lauderdale, FL 33316
      - **Contact**: +1 954-525-2421
      - A lively waterfront restaurant serving fresh seafood, like oysters and mahi-mahi, with stunning views of the marina.
  - **Louie Bossi's**
      - **Address**: 1032 E Las Olas Blvd, Fort Lauderdale, FL 33301
      - **Contact**: +1 954-356-6699
      - A chic Italian bistro known for its handmade pastas, wood-fired pizzas, and vibrant outdoor courtyard.

- **Things to Do**:
  - **Kayaking the Canals**: Rent a kayak or paddleboard and glide through Fort Lauderdale's extensive canal system, often called the "Venice of America." You'll pass by luxurious homes, swaying palm trees, and serene waters.
  - **Explore Hugh Taylor Birch State Park**: A tranquil escape right in the heart of the city. Hike or

bike along nature trails, kayak in the lagoon, or have a picnic under the shady trees.
- **Sunset Cruises**: Join a guided boat tour in the evening to soak up the stunning colors of the sunset over the waterways. Many tours include live music and refreshments.

Riverwalk Arts & Entertainment District: Stroll along this scenic promenade that connects museums, theaters, and trendy restaurants.

2. Key West

A lively island escape with a laid-back atmosphere, Key West is the southernmost point in the United States and is famous for its unique culture, breathtaking sunsets, and vibrant nightlife.

- **Key Attractions**:
    - **Duval Street**: This lively street is a hub of activity, featuring vibrant bars, unique shops, and eclectic restaurants. Stop by the historic Sloppy Joe's Bar for live music and a taste of local flavor.
    - **Ernest Hemingway Home & Museum**: Tour the historic home of the legendary author and meet the descendants of his famous six-toed cats. The lush gardens and insightful stories make it a must-visit.
    - **Mallory Square**: Every evening, Mallory Square comes alive with its Sunset Celebration, where you can enjoy street performers, artists, and vendors while watching the sun dip below the horizon.
    - **Fort Zachary Taylor State Park**: Explore the historic Civil War-era fort or relax on the sandy beaches, perfect for swimming, snorkeling, and picnicking.
- **Coordinates**: 24.5551° N, 81.7799° W
- **Hotels**:
    - **The Casablanca Hotel**

- **Address**: 904 Duval St, Key West, FL 33040
- **Contact**: +1 305-296-0815
- A charming boutique hotel with tropical-themed rooms, located right on Duval Street. Rates start at ~$130/night.
  - **Blue Marlin Motel**
    - **Address**: 1320 Simonton St, Key West, FL 33040
    - **Contact**: +1 305-294-2585
    - A budget-friendly option with a retro vibe, an outdoor pool, and spacious rooms. Rates start at ~$150/night.
- **Restaurants**:
  - **Blue Heaven**
    - **Address**: 729 Thomas St, Key West, FL 33040
    - **Contact**: +1 305-296-8666
    - A quirky outdoor eatery offering Caribbean-inspired dishes like lobster Benedict and conch fritters. Known for its vibrant atmosphere and famous Key lime pie.
  - **El Siboney**
    - **Address**: 900 Catherine St, Key West, FL 33040
    - **Contact**: +1 305-296-4184
    - A local favorite serving authentic Cuban dishes, such as ropa vieja and flavorful black beans.
- **Things to Do**:
  - **Snorkeling & Diving**: Immerse yourself in the crystal-clear waters, where you can discover vibrant coral reefs full of diverse marine life. Whether you're snorkeling just beneath the surface or diving deeper, you'll be captivated by the colorful underwater world, with its abundance of fish, corals, and other sea creatures, offering an unforgettable experience for nature lovers and

adventure seekers alike. Key West offers several guided tours, perfect for beginners and experienced divers alike.
- **Conch Train Tour**: Hop aboard this charming open-air train to learn about the island's rich history, colorful characters, and architectural gems.
- **Key West Butterfly & Nature Conservatory**: Step into an enchanting glass-enclosed garden teeming with vibrant butterflies and exotic birds, creating a serene and magical experience.
- **Southernmost Point Buoy**: Don't miss the opportunity to snap a memorable photo at this iconic landmark, which marks the southernmost point of the continental United States. Situated just 90 miles from Cuba, it's a must-see destination for visitors, offering a unique chance to stand at the very tip of the U.S. and take in the stunning surroundings while commemorating a truly remarkable spot.

3. Naples

Known for its luxury and natural beauty, Naples is a Gulf Coast gem offering pristine beaches, world-class dining, and a tranquil atmosphere perfect for relaxation.

- **Key Attractions**:
    - **Naples Pier**: A historic spot ideal for dolphin spotting and enjoying breathtaking sunsets over the Gulf of Mexico. It's also a popular place for fishing enthusiasts.
    - **Third Street South & Fifth Avenue South**: These elegant shopping districts are brimming with charming boutiques, fine dining, and quaint sidewalk cafes.
    - **Corkscrew Swamp Sanctuary**: A nature lover's paradise with a 2.5-mile boardwalk that winds through wetlands, cypress forests, and diverse

wildlife habitats. Bring binoculars for birdwatching!
- **Coordinates**: 26.1420° N, 81.7948° W
- **Hotels**:
  - **Inn on Fifth**
    - **Address**: 699 5th Ave S, Naples, FL 34102
    - **Contact**: +1 239-403-8777
    - A sophisticated boutique hotel offering rooftop hot tubs and easy access to Fifth Avenue dining and shopping. Rates start at ~$200/night.
  - **Trianon Old Naples**
    - **Address**: 955 7th Ave S, Naples, FL 34102
    - **Contact**: +1 239-435-9600
    - A charming, budget-friendly hotel with an Old Florida vibe, located near the historic district. Rates start at ~$140/night.
- **Restaurants**:
  - **The Dock at Crayton Cove**
    - **Address**: 845 12th Ave S, Naples, FL 34102
    - **Contact**: +1 239-263-9940
    - A laid-back waterfront spot offering fresh seafood and tropical cocktails, with views of Naples Bay.
  - **Campiello**
    - **Address**: 1177 3rd St S, Naples, FL 34102
    - **Contact**: +1 239-435-1166
    - Located in a historic building, this Italian restaurant is renowned for its wood-fired pizzas and flavorful pasta dishes.
- **Things to Do**:
  - **Kayaking & Paddleboarding**: Rent a kayak to explore the mangroves at Delnor-Wiggins Pass State Park. The calm waters are perfect for spotting manatees and tropical fish.
  - **Visit the Naples Zoo**: A family-friendly attraction featuring exotic animals, interactive exhibits, and a unique primate boat tour.

- o **Explore the Naples Botanical Garden**: A 170-acre paradise showcasing plants from around the globe. The garden is a haven for nature lovers and a vibrant venue for seasonal events and art installations. Year-round, visitors can enjoy unique exhibitions and festive celebrations, ensuring there's always something new to experience.
- o **Luxury Shopping**: Stroll through Waterside Shops, a high-end outdoor mall with designer stores and fine dining options.

4. Sarasota

Sarasota offers a rich blend of art, culture, and spectacular beaches, making it a favorite for travelers seeking both relaxation and inspiration.

- **Key Attractions**:
  - o **The Ringling Museum**: A cultural treasure featuring art galleries, the Ca' d'Zan Mansion, and beautifully landscaped gardens. Dive into Sarasota's rich history with a captivating look at the world of the circus and its cultural significance.
  - o **Siesta Key Beach:** Renowned as one of the top beaches in the U.S., it boasts pristine white sand and crystal-clear turquoise waters that offer an unparalleled coastal experience.
  - o **Marie Selby Botanical Gardens**: A lush, bayfront garden showcasing tropical plants, orchids, and tranquil walking paths. The views of Sarasota Bay are breathtaking.
- **Coordinates**: 27.3364° N, 82.5307° W
- **Hotels**:
  - o **Aloft Sarasota**
    - **Address**: 1401 Ringling Blvd, Sarasota, FL 34236
    - **Contact**: +1 941-870-0900

- A modern, pet-friendly hotel with a rooftop pool and easy access to downtown Sarasota. Rates start at ~$150/night.
  - **Siesta Key Palms Resort**
    - **Address**: 1800 Stickney Point Rd, Sarasota, FL 34231
    - **Contact**: +1 941-684-3244
    - A tropical retreat offering cozy rooms, hammocks, and proximity to Siesta Key Beach. Rates start at ~$130/night.
- **Restaurants**:
  - **Owen's Fish Camp**
    - **Address**: 516 Burns Ct, Sarasota, FL 34236
    - **Contact**: +1 941-951-6936
    - A casual Southern-style seafood joint in a historic cottage, serving fresh fish and craft beers.
  - **Shore**
    - **Address**: 465 John Ringling Blvd, Sarasota, FL 34236
    - **Contact**: +1 941-296-0301
    - A trendy eatery offering modern beach-inspired cuisine, with great cocktails and waterfront seating.
- **Things to Do**:
  - **Sunset Cruise**: Book a tour with Marina Jack to watch the sunset over Sarasota Bay. Many cruises include dining and live music.
  - **Explore the Rosemary District**: This vibrant arts district is filled with unique galleries, murals, and local boutiques.
  - **Visit Mote Marine Laboratory**: An interactive marine science center featuring sharks, sea turtles, and other marine life. Kids will love the hands-on exhibits.
  - **Attend a Performance**: Sarasota Opera and Van Wezel Performing Arts Hall regularly host world-

class performances, from opera to Broadway shows.

5. Islamorada (Florida Keys)

Islamorada, known as the "Sportfishing Capital of the World," is a tropical paradise with a laid-back atmosphere and endless opportunities for outdoor adventures.

- **Key Attractions**:
    - **Theater of the Sea**: A marine park where visitors can swim with dolphins, sea lions, and even sharks. The lush tropical setting makes it an unforgettable experience.
    - **Robbie's Marina**: A must-visit spot to hand-feed giant tarpon fish and enjoy fresh seafood at the on-site restaurant.
    - **Windley Key Fossil Reef Geological State Park**: A fascinating park showcasing fossilized coral reefs and trails through native vegetation.
- **Coordinates**: 24.9240° N, 80.6276° W
- **Hotels**:
    - **Islander Resort**
        - **Address**: 82100 Overseas Hwy, Islamorada, FL 33036
        - **Contact**: +1 305-664-2031
        - A family-friendly beachfront resort with cottages and outdoor activities. Rates start at ~$180/night.
    - **Amara Cay Resort**
        - **Address**: 80001 Overseas Hwy, Islamorada, FL 33036
        - **Contact**: +1 305-664-0073
        - A stylish, oceanfront property with a poolside tiki bar and modern rooms. Rates start at ~$190/night.
- **Restaurants**:
    - **Lazy Days**

- **Address**: 79867 Overseas Hwy, Islamorada, FL 33036
                - **Contact**: +1 305-664-5256
                - A casual spot serving fresh seafood, with outdoor seating overlooking the ocean.
            - **Morada Bay**
                - **Address**: 81600 Overseas Hwy, Islamorada, FL 33036
                - **Contact**: +1 305-664-0604
                - A beach café perfect for sunset dinners, offering Caribbean-inspired dishes and stunning ocean views.
    - **Things to Do**:
        - **Deep-Sea Fishing**: Book a fishing charter to reel in mahi-mahi, tuna, or sailfish. Islamorada is a haven for anglers of all skill levels.
        - **Glass-Bottom Boat Tour**: Explore the vibrant coral reefs without getting wet. These tours are ideal for families and offer spectacular views of marine life.
        - **History of Diving Museum**: Learn about the evolution of underwater exploration through fascinating exhibits and artifacts.
        - **Paddleboarding & Kayaking**: Rent gear to explore the calm, crystal-clear waters around the mangroves. It's a peaceful way to spot wildlife like manatees and sea turtles.

6. Delray Beach

Delray Beach is a charming coastal town that blends a beautiful shoreline with a vibrant cultural scene. Known for its artsy atmosphere, it attracts visitors who appreciate both nature and creativity.

- **Key Attractions**:
    - **Atlantic Avenue**: The heart of Delray Beach, this bustling street is lined with boutique shops, cafes,

restaurants, and art galleries. Whether you're shopping for unique souvenirs, dining in style, or enjoying the nightlife, there's something for everyone.
    - **Delray Beach Public Beach**: This beach is an ideal destination for sunbathing, swimming, or unwinding. With its tranquil waters and relaxed atmosphere, it's perfect for both families and couples looking to enjoy a peaceful day by the sea.
    - **Morikami Museum and Japanese Gardens**: A peaceful retreat that immerses visitors in Japanese culture through meticulously curated gardens, exhibits, and tea ceremonies.
- **Coordinates**: 26.4610° N, 80.0728° W
- **Hotels**:
    - **The Seagate Hotel & Spa**
        - **Address**: 1000 E Atlantic Ave, Delray Beach, FL 33483
        - **Contact**: +1 561-665-4800
        - A luxurious boutique hotel with a beautiful pool, golf course, and a renowned spa. Ideal for those seeking a relaxing stay with easy access to the beach. Rates start at ~$350/night.
    - **Colony Hotel & Cabaña Club**
        - **Address**: 525 E Atlantic Ave, Delray Beach, FL 33483
        - **Contact**: +1 561-278-4567
        - A historic property known for its art deco design and prime location near the beach and shops. The Colony offers a cozy, boutique feel with a beachfront cabana club. Rates start at ~$200/night.
- **Restaurants**:
    - **Café L'Europe**
        - **Address**: 331 E Atlantic Ave, Delray Beach, FL 33483
        - **Contact**: +1 561-274-1000

- A fine dining institution in Delray Beach offering European-inspired cuisine with a focus on fresh seafood. The elegant atmosphere makes it perfect for romantic dinners or special occasions.
    - o **The Sundy House**
        - **Address**: 106 S Swinton Ave, Delray Beach, FL 33444
        - **Contact**: +1 561-272-5678
        - A historic mansion set in a lush tropical garden, serving a delicious fusion of Caribbean and American flavors. The garden setting offers a unique dining experience.
- **Things to Do**:
    - o **Delray Beach Arts District**: Take a stroll through this vibrant district filled with art galleries, murals, and performance venues. Don't miss the "First Friday Art Walk" for a unique local experience.
    - o **Visit the Sandoway Discovery Center**: A great spot for families, this interactive center offers hands-on exhibits focused on marine life, including touch tanks and wildlife exhibits.
    - o **Explore the Pineapple Grove Arts District**: Known for its eclectic mix of art studios, boutiques, and cafes, this district is perfect for a leisurely afternoon of exploring.
    - o **Catch Live Music at a Local Venue**: From jazz to rock, Delray Beach's music scene offers plenty of opportunities to hear local talent at venues like the Arts Garage.

7. Homestead

Homestead serves as the gateway to some of Florida's most iconic natural wonders, making it a must-visit for outdoor enthusiasts. Located just south of Miami, it offers a range of adventures perfect for nature lovers and thrill-seekers.

- **Key Attractions**:
    - **Everglades National Park**: A UNESCO World Heritage site, the Everglades is home to one of the planet's most distinctive and rare ecosystems. Explore vast wetlands teeming with alligators, manatees, and a wide range of bird species. Airboat tours offer a thrilling way to navigate through the swamps.
    - **Biscayne National Park**: A marine paradise offering crystal-clear waters perfect for snorkeling, diving, and kayaking. Explore coral reefs and shipwrecks in this aquatic haven.
    - **Coral Castle**: Discover the intriguing story behind Coral Castle, an extraordinary, hand-crafted stone structure created by Edward Leedskalnin, a solitary man who used massive coral rocks to build this remarkable monument. Despite its mystery—since Leedskalnin never revealed how he moved and shaped the enormous stones—this captivating site stands as a testament to his incredible ingenuity and dedication. Visitors can marvel at the precision and artistry of the structure, which continues to inspire wonder and fascination. The origin of the castle's construction remains a mystery, and it's a fascinating stop for history buffs and puzzle lovers.
- **Coordinates**: 25.4687° N, 80.4771° W
- **Hotels**:
    - **Floridian Hotel**
        - **Address**: 990 N Homestead Blvd, Homestead, FL 33030
        - **Contact**: +1 305-247-4110
        - A charming, budget-friendly hotel with clean rooms and a relaxing atmosphere, ideal for travelers exploring the Everglades. Rates start at ~$90/night.
    - **Hampton Inn & Suites Miami-South/Homestead**
        - **Address**: 2855 NE 9th St, Homestead, FL 33033

- **Contact**: +1 305-257-9999
- A modern and comfortable hotel offering free breakfast and a pool, conveniently located near the entrance to Everglades National Park. Rates start at ~$130/night.

- **Restaurants**:
    - **Robert is Here**
        - **Address**: 19200 SW 344th St, Homestead, FL 33034
        - **Contact**: +1 305-246-1592
        - Famous for its fresh fruit milkshakes, Robert is Here also serves local produce and has a unique farmstand feel.
    - **The Fish House**
        - **Address**: 1035 N Krome Ave, Homestead, FL 33030
        - **Contact**: +1 305-248-0039
        - A no-frills seafood restaurant known for its fresh fish and key lime pie. It's a great place to relax after a day of adventure.

- **Things to Do**:
    - **Explore Everglades National Park**: Experience the wilderness of the Everglades on an airboat tour or take a guided walking tour through the park's diverse ecosystems. Be sure to spot alligators and exotic birds along the way!
    - **Visit the Fruit and Spice Park**: This unique park offers a chance to sample rare tropical fruits and explore lush gardens filled with fruit-bearing plants.
    - **Go Kayaking at Biscayne National Park**: Paddle through the crystal-clear waters, exploring hidden coves and coral reefs teeming with marine life.
    - **Discover Coral Castle**: Unravel the mystery of this architectural wonder, built entirely out of coral rock by one man with incredible precision.

FINAL THOUGHTS

Embark on Your Florida Adventure with Confidence

It's clear that Florida is more than just a vacation destination: it's a state bursting with contrasts, diversity, and endless opportunities for discovery.

While iconic destinations like Miami, Orlando, and the Florida Keys attract millions of visitors, the heart of Florida lies in the places that don't always make the headlines. Whether you're meandering through the Spanish colonial streets of St. Augustine, savoring fresh seafood in Cedar Key, or standing in awe of the natural beauty of the Everglades, Florida's charm lies in the details—the unexpected, the unique, and the truly unforgettable.

This guide is not just a checklist of places to visit; it's an invitation to immerse yourself in the Sunshine State's vibrant culture, its stories, and its history. It inspires you to look beyond the obvious and immerse yourself in Florida's rich cultural tapestry. Every trip here is a chance to forge meaningful connections with the landscape, its communities, and its heritage.

It's about discovering that a road trip down U.S. 1 is not just a drive but a rite of passage. That sitting by a Gulf Coast sunset feels different from any other sunset. That wandering through Florida's springs, beaches, or small-town festivals leaves you with a deep appreciation for its diversity.

Remember, the beauty of Florida lies not just in what you see but in how it makes you feel. It's the warmth of the sun on your face, the sound of waves lapping against the shore, the thrill of spotting wildlife, and the laughter shared with loved ones over a plate of fresh Key Lime pie. It's these moments that make the journey worthwhile and the memories that linger long after the trip is over.

So, as you close this book and begin planning your adventure, let it remind you that travel is about more than destinations—it's about curiosity, connection, and stepping outside your routine to experience something extraordinary. Florida offers countless possibilities, but the real magic happens when you embrace the unexpected, take a detour, and let yourself be enchanted by the journey.

Here's to your Florida adventure—a story waiting to be written, a memory waiting to be made, and a journey that promises to be as vibrant, diverse, and unforgettable as the state itself. Safe travels!

Download your FREE digital copy of the Florida Bucket List for easy access anytime!

© Copyright 2024 Dylan and Rachel Marston All rights reserved

Made in the USA
Las Vegas, NV
25 February 2025